TAG

TANGIBLE ACTION GUIDE

FOR REAL ESTATE MARKETING

Matt Muscat

NOTE FROM THE AUTHOR

"To all those who I have met with over the years, thank you for teaching me. To all of those who I have not yet met with, I look forward to learning together."

—Matt Muscat

If you are reading this, you have made it past a quote by me, and are probably wondering if you should keep going. The time you spend reading this book is time you are risking on my ideas when you could be doing literally anything else. I want you to know that I respect your time. The ideas in this book fit a pattern, they are tangible and actionable. They are not perfect, some will be your style and some will not. There is however power in variety, and power in the imperfect because "a plan today" is always better than waiting for "the perfect plan tomorrow". The strategies in this book are all ones that you can read and execute at the same time with a little creativity.

TABLE OF CONTENTS

FOREWORD

By Kevin Polakovich

I met Matt Muscat in 2011, at the time he was finishing his master's degree from Michigan State University. It was obvious from the first meeting he was not a typical student graduating from academia. When I say that, I mean that he is not someone who finished school and thought they had it all figured out just because they spent a lot of money over many years learning theories and ideas. From the day we started working together I saw in Matt a quest for knowledge, I also saw someone with the ability to look at successful outcomes and engineer simple plans of how to recreate the desired results. For over 20 years in my sales career, I have had the privilege (mostly) to attend countless seminars about how to do this or be that. Most leave you with an enthusiasm to tackle the world, to change your life, to be the best you that you can be... that feeling is typically fleeting because it lacks actionable tasks that will lead you to your desired outcome.

Getting to and staying at the top in the real estate industry is all about a PLAN and EXECUTION. Matt delivers real-world ideas and a PLAN that can help you achieve success at a very high level, but it is up to you EXECUTE.

Kevin Polakovich is a top producing mortgage loan officer and founder of Treadstone Funding. Kevin has been ranked in the top 20 nationally for personal mortgage sales in the United States by the Scotsman Guide and currently averages over 100 million dollars in annual sales. He is a national mortgage coach for other top lenders through the CORE, and is also a successful real estate investor.

INTRODUCTION

Does it ever feel like all of the successful sales people around you are simply pulling business out of thin air? There's a good reason that it can look that way to many people. The best sales people are! No, they aren't getting deals through witchcraft or wizardry, and to my knowledge, there is no Hogwarts School of Sales Trickery. These expert sales pros are exerting forces that allow them (your colleagues and competitors who make sales look easy) to get business out of any interaction they are a part of, thus casting the illusion that their leads are coming out of thin air.

When I was 7 years old, I started my first business. It was called the "Morning Mouthful" (my friends now mercilessly tease me because of the imagery that moniker now elicits in their dark minds). It was a newspaper with my funny take on the news and current events. I would make one issue per week and sell copies to classmates and friends for fifty cents. At the peak, I was making over $8/week —an almost unfathomable amount of money for me and many of my friends at the time. It wasn't that I had a product that sold itself, or that the pricing was so low that everyone bought it. People bought my paper because I asked. People bought it because I "sold" it. I created the demand. Although we will cover creating your own demand much later, this set the stage for future endeavors and even this book.

Years later, when I worked in retail sales at a local shopping mall, the same concepts of asking for sales and creating demand were again illuminated. I didn't work at an ultra-competitive store, but many weeks myself and another talented sales associate were able to win various sales contests by simply talking to more customers. I knew next to nothing about fashion, in fact at the time I was still wearing gym socks with dress shoes (a trend that very sadly continued into my career in real estate until a colleague politely suggested a change). What I did know is that if I folded clothes in the front of the store, I would be positioned in such a spot that I could be the first team member to greet shoppers walking in. By getting the most greetings, I could start to develop the most relationships. Knowing little about clothes I always tried to make conversation about anything else. This turned out to be a big advantage because it made my style less salesy than other colleagues. After developing some rapport I would let shoppers know about any promotion that was happening and inform them that I would be around if they needed, but that I wouldn't bother them (often going so far as to make the joke about how annoying overbearing sales people at furniture stores can be).

I would then work on other projects and help other customers while ensuring that I was present. When my customers then began to engage with the merchandise in more than just a browsing type way, I would bring them a bottle of water. The goal here was to keep people longer. Our store was genius at the time and figured out that once you give someone something of value they often feel slightly more obligated to engage longer. Sometimes this engaging led to a conversation and other times it led to purchases. Either way, it was a great way to further a customer's relationship with the brand, and with me. It was just a bottle of water. It was simple.

If the customer advanced past looking around and wanted to try something on I would suggest another article of clothing or accessory that paired well with their original item, often remarking that "The last shopper actually wore this shirt underneath this cardigan and it looked great!" This would then give me a higher chance of selling multiple items by placing new ideas in people's heads. Although I hadn't heard it at the time, this quote now makes perfect sense when I reflect back: "You miss 100% of the shots you never take." —Wayne Gretzky.

In the same simple way that by asking people to buy my newspaper I could sell more copies, by simply talking to more customers and giving suggestions of more things that they could purchase, I could make more sales. It seemed too easy.

By the time I got into the real estate industry in 2011, the concepts of asking for business and figuring out simple strategies were still swimming around in my head. At first real estate seemed harder. I wasn't selling a newspaper for quarters and my office was competing for the same customers that some of the biggest banks and brokerages in the world were. Yet month after month business would grow. The ideas we used weren't overly complicated. My mentors taught me their strategies of asking for business from Realtors, past clients, friends, family etc. They taught me to offer simple value, and to develop relationships. A few months in and I couldn't believe it. Getting a customer to choose to work with you for their $250,000 purchase was, in essence, the same simple process as getting a friend to buy a newspaper or getting a mall walker to shop with you. All sales based industries, it would seem, have opportunity and value simplicity.

These ideas turned into a thought process that I now live by because they can be applied to any situation, sales based or otherwise. There is opportunity (and money if that is your goal) literally everywhere you look. Those who find the best ways to execute on these opportunities will succeed. The best part is that the 'pie' (defined here as opportunity) is big, those who play the 'game' (the game of life or business) strategically can create their own demand and as a result their own successes out of thin air, hard work, hopes, goals, and dreams. The last things in that line are all things that, for the most part, are free to those with a little grit and creativity.

Early Apologies: After re-reading the above two paragraphs a couple times the inner sales person in me started to hate this book already. How could I possibly hate my own book? So many books about sales and business in general focus all on motivation, positive thinking, and hard work. These books mainly teach in generalities and although they may pump you up, they don't often give you exact directions, they lack tangibility. Inevitably after reading these types of books, the reader gets excited, then gets busy and goes back to real life without having anything real to implement. All of a sudden everything the reader learned is forgotten until the next time things slow down and they inevitably attend the next conference or read the next book. This exact thing has happened to me countless times, and I wanted to write a guide that would be different. I wanted to put together a book that would be a mirror to the meetings I have with other real estate professionals where we simply go into detail about what is working, and how to solve specific problems. For that exact reason, some of the ideas in here may seem conversationally written, and not as buttoned up as you would normally see in a book. The content to come is a compilation of guides I give to other sales people, and guides some have given to me.

Make no mistake, I am not saying that you shouldn't attend conferences or read motivational sales books. Every once and a while we all need a little pick me up, but there are enough of those books, speakers, and presenters out there already, and I wanted to offer up something different.

I want this book to be tangible and usable for real estate industry sales people with even the shortest of attention spans. Seriously. I wrote this book for me, partially as a way to organize all of the things I say to those I coach, and partially to create an audience. It is my hope that readers join together on social media to take the ideas in this book and adapt and share them, adding new strategies whenever possible.

The name TAG is no mistake and is not just an acronym. TAG is a tangible action guide for real estate professionals. Tag is also a children's game that has rules that are ridiculously simple. The relation between the two is no accident because all of the best marketing should be simple. Often times simple also translates into short so TAG is written in short chapters, and the entire guide is itself shorter than many other longer winded business tomes. Before we had the title, my editor actually dubbed TAG the "choose your own adventure guide for real estate" because a sales person can flip to any chapter, find an idea that looks good to them, and turn it into lead generating or life simplifying action within minutes. No two people reading TAG are likely to resonate with the same set of ideas or execute them in the same way. Even if they did, the "adventures" would likely play out very differently because all sales people have different audiences.

TAG's goal is to focus not only on big trends and digital marketing, but also on ways to adapt and supplement traditional marketing techniques for use in the digital world. Every reader is different, and different things work in different markets, so you will also see topics like improving your door knocking game, and how to mail more effectively.

So where is all of this information coming from? And why am I the guy you should listen to? Since 2011, I have been meeting with real estate agents, lenders, insurance agents, title account executives, and have been soaking up information on what works and what doesn't when it comes to lead generation and business growth. Some strategies will be ones my team generated, and others will be those that were shared with us. Other tactics have been borrowed and adapted from different industries, but tested and found to work in real estate. Some tactics will work for large teams but many of them can also work or be tweaked for solo agents/or lenders who are new to their market and who don't have a large marketing budget. I interviewed both top mortgage loan officers and Realtors and sought their expertise to figure out exactly what they were doing to generate business both now and at the beginning of their careers. In a real estate industry that is changing and shifting every day, where many sales professionals have become dependent on expensive and often unreliable online leads, TAG strives to be a guide to deepen your arsenal of strategies and put you back in control of your business.

Before we can even start talking about what marketing techniques you can use to get business, we first have to set some ground rules.

SECTION 1

TIME
BLOCKING

———

Time Blocking 101: Just Do It

The one thing that all of the strategies and tactics in this book will have in common is that none of them will work if you don't schedule time for them. Execution is everything.

You must (I repeat) MUST time block.

If your schedule doesn't currently allow for marketing/lead generation, and the number one reason why you're not doing a lot of marketing is that you truly "don't have time", no amount of tips in this book can help you. Plain and simple. Your schedule has to have openings in order to make this book work. Trust me, many people who close a lot more sales than you also have more time than you. None of us are as busy as we think.

Understand What Time Blocking Isn't

Time blocking does not mean:

- You abandon your family
- You stop exercising
- You stop doing all the things that matter to you

I am not going to lead generate or market at the expense of missing out on special time with my family. My wife is far too beautiful, and my son is way too cute. No exercise? No way, you can't have a healthy business without a healthy lifestyle, plus without the gym what would you even brag about on Instagram? You simply can not stop doing all of the things that matter to you or make you happy and try to replace them with work. Even if you love your job, it is a recipe for failure. Time blocking should be done the same way that all good things in life are, in moderation.

The most effective way to time block your marketing and lead generation is to do so in a way that helps you better organize all aspects of your life, not just work. Time block the gym. Time block date night and family time. Heck, time block video games if that is important to your mental health.

Pick Days And Times That Make Sense For You And The Strategy

When we talk about time blocking, it is really important to pick days in your calendar that are not going to overwhelm you. What I mean is that if you always have to drop your kid off at school at 8 in the morning, then 8 am to 10 am isn't a realistic time to put aside for prospecting. Similarly, if you are always starving at 7:30 am and always take your morning restroom trip after your coffee at 7:45 then listen to your body and schedule around it.

Think about the times of day that you are most productive. The times when you can dedicate the longest, most productive swaths of time and when you can be in a location that makes sense for the work you are scheduling. Over time I have learned that 8:45 am-11:00 am is my best time for getting projects done (especially any project or task that I am not excited about) as well as any creative work. If I need to get this type of work done again later in the day typically I wait until 8 pm when the day's distractions are often behind me and my son is in bed. Does this mean that I only work for 2-4 hours per day? No, I simply schedule activities during the other times that fit where I know my body and mind will be. I am always hungry around 11:45 am and thus that time is reserved for lunch meetings. If you are mentally exhausted every day by 3 pm, schedule your gym time, or a trip to the coffee shop.

We all work differently and have different environmental, social, and emotional needs. Find the times in your calendar where you are most likely to complete, stick to, and overall be successful at the things you choose to time block.

Start With Three

Starting time blocking initially can be tough. Scheduling out 16 of your 24 hours a day with specific activities and no wiggle room for life can often be a recipe for failure. I like to tell people to start by picking three days a week and within those days to pick different times for blocked out activities. When it comes to time blocking meetings, you can leave time in your blocks for meetings ahead of time without getting specific on who the meetings will be with. This will also help you to not use meetings as a way to schedule "something more important" over other time blocked activities.

The Timing Of Time Blocking: Be Cognizant Of Other People's Schedules

Remember what your mother taught you?

My mom always said it is rude to call people after 9 pm (granted that was back when home phones without a vibrate mode were still a thing). Nobody will like you if you irritate them. This does change for people you have existing relationships with: the more you know about your clients or prospects, the more flexible you can be. In general, time block your calls at times when it will be convenient for the person on the other end.

Maybe you have a 2nd job or you really only have time to do your prospecting activity at night. One trick many sales professionals use is to send 10 text messages out earlier in the day to people who they want to schedule prospecting calls or follow-ups with later at night. Let the recipient know that you can call back at "X time" if it isn't too late for them. The beauty of this tactic is that it makes prospecting that much easier by setting an agreed upon date and time when your subject will answer the phone. By putting 5-10 minutes into texting earlier in the day, a savvy sales person can stack their "time block" full of scheduled calls with prospects who are already committed to and available for a conversation.

Another alternative if your time doesn't allow for prospecting until the evening and you don't want to make calls too late, is to utilize social media. Although it might be awkward and annoying to call people after 9 pm, a late night Facebook message doesn't carry the same social taboo. The ability of the end user to choose when to answer your message makes it more okay to send late, and in fact, a non-work day message may actually break through the noise and not come off as salesy. We will cover Facebook marketing using Messenger more extensively in a later chapter.

Didn't Write It? Didn't Type It? Didn't Set It? — It Won't Happen!

If it isn't written or typed out somewhere in a calendar, or scheduled in your customer relationship management (CRM) system, it does not exist. A task is not real if it is not written down. Even the act of putting a task in your calendar/planner/iPhone/Trapper Keeper[1] or Palm Pilot[2] makes you more likely to complete the task.

Need an extra push? Add someone else to the task to keep you accountable. People perform better when they know others are watching.[3] This idea of time blocking with accountability partners works especially well as a team strategy.

Time Blocking On A Daily, Weekly, Monthly, And Yearly Schedule

There are many activities I am going to cover in this book that you need to do every day or every other day, but some things you only need to time block for a couple times per week, per month, and/or per year. It is important to put all of these action items into your schedule now. Stealing the 'word' of the eloquent rapper Warren G — time blocking days, weeks, months and even quarters out will help you "regulate".

If you are a sales person or are self-employed, a lot of times when you "go into work" in the morning, it's hard to figure out what you need to be doing. If every day you "get into work mode" and have to think about what you could do to be productive, you haven't time blocked enough productive activities. One of the number one reasons many self-employed people never get consistently busy is because they are terrible at time management and slow days cascade from snowflakes into an avalanche, and before you know it you have an open calendar and no pipeline for future business.

---

[1] Trapper Keeper: A prehistoric device that became popular among students in the late 1970's and early 1980's for organizing and storing notes, due dates, and folders.
[2] Palm Pilot. Lol.
[3] Phenomena called the Hawthorne Effect also known as the Observer Effect. A type of re-activity in which individuals modify their behavior when others are thought to be watching.

Monthly: Review Your Time Blocking

It is important to schedule a monthly review to see how well you completed your task list and to measure the successes or re-evaluate. Time block into your schedule 15 minutes on one Friday a month to see how many time blocks you stuck to, what percentage did you accomplish, and what were the results? Measuring success can be tricky, but any plan today is better than a perfect plan tomorrow, and the next section covers a common method that people set for measuring success.

How To Measure Time Blocking Success

For many marketing and prospecting tasks in real estate, it can take 2-3 months to see a closing. This can be such a long time that many people lose focus on their time blocking because they don't see immediate "closed" results. Thus closings might not be the best measure of success, especially in the short term. Many activities you time block may be considered successful if they simply generate a sales lead, deepen a relationship, help to convert a lead, or save you time. Look back at the things you did two months ago and write down what they led to. Once you are able to measure success you will also be more likely to stick to your endeavors and better prune & refine your activities.

How Many Hours Should You Be Time Blocking Per Week?

This is all going to depend on your industry AND how much more business you are looking to get. What becomes important is to be able to do the math and work backwards.

For instance, if you get 10 leads and you close two of them, you make 'z' dollars, how many hours did it take you to generate those leads? If you are able to figure out, for example, that 10 hours of marketing gets you 'x' amount of leads, 'y' amount of closings, and 'z' amount of a paycheck, then it becomes easier to figure out how much time you should be putting into your marketing time block.

You can time block for anything in your life. In fact, anything that is important in your life you should be time blocking for. The more you are able to time block with some buffers for fun time and the unexpected, the more likely it is that you will hit your marks without feeling overwhelmed. I'm literally ending this paragraph here because my 9 pm time block calls for bourbon and Netflix.

Finally, time blocking is important even if your entire schedule is open. This is because time blocking sets you up for success in the future by guaranteeing that your most valuable asset—time—is always available and reserved for the right types of activities. Simply put, without time blocks, your time will disappear. As your time gets more and more valuable, the value you will get from time blocking will grow exponentially.

ACCOUNTABILITY

————

Accountability 101

Time blocking is important, but what is equally, if not more important is accountability.

Time and time again I see that people who are accountable to others (not just themselves) are more successful in everything they work on. Sure, some people are personally motivated even without the help of others, but even they usually benefit from accountability. If you are among the millions of others who need a little extra push to get through the day, having an accountability partner in the same or a similar industry can be huge. In the same way that there are thousands of flavors of ice cream, there are many types of accountability partners and what is important is that you figure out which flavor is right for you.

Accountability Coaches

A trending way to keep accountable lately is by having a coach. Someone who is leaps and bounds ahead of you can keep you accountable, share tips and tricks, and inspire you by giving you new ideas. You are hiring them because they have already been where you are planning to go, and can fill in some of the blanks in addition to holding your feet to the fire. A professional coach can be a great resource and a great way to not feel alone on your "sales island." If you go this route in hiring a coach, I highly recommend you find someone with relevant, recent, or current experience and not just a self-proclaimed coach (who are typically people who can't sell themselves). You want someone who has been where you want to be. Someone who is experienced in modern times and understands the fundamentals of your industry. Looking for the best coach? Talk to the 10 best sales people in your market (or a different market) and see who comes recommended. See who your broker recommends, and ask to see results from people they coached. This type of professional coaching can be expensive, but well worth it. I have seen real estate coaching programs ranging from $60/hr to $3,000/mo. I usually wouldn't advocate something this expensive, but having seen multiple 20 million dollars per year sales people reach the 50 and 100 million dollar levels after 2 years of coaching, I'd say the proof is in the pudding.

Warning: *Professional coaching only works if you buy in fully, and listen to your coach.*

Accountability Peers

If you want accountability but aren't ready to make a financial investment, one great option is to get an accountability peer/partner. We all learn in different ways. Some people respond and learn better from a peer who is in the trenches with them rather than a coach who preaches from a seemingly unachievable mountain top. It can be rewarding to find someone who is on the same level as you are, so that you can continually meet and keep each other accountable while bouncing ideas and back and forth. You and your accountability peer can even meet together and do some of your time blocking, emailing, phone calls, etc at the same time. You can learn how they market with their pitch, instead of feeling like you are on an island all alone. Their small victories can become yours and can help you both develop at twice the speed. Your relationship with your accountability partner needs to be symbiotic. You want the level of value received to be high for all parties involved.

 Every couple of months or years it can also be good to switch partners and find someone who can introduce you to new ideas. If you are committed to your partner and both want to stay together, consider having a ménage à trois[4] by inviting someone new to one of your sessions.

Setting Accountability Rewards

What if you are like the millions of people out there who have tried being accountable before but are never able to stick to it? You get a great idea, you go to a conference, you are inspired, and then... it quickly fades away. One way around this is to set rewards for both small and big goals. Most people only do big goals, but if this hasn't worked for you in the past, try setting mini goals along the way. Sure buying a black Mercedes when you earn your first 6 figure income can sound like it

---

[4] My editor suggested adding a footnote here with a definition for anyone who is unfamiliar with the term. I think most of you will get it, but if not, please don't hold me responsible for what pulls up on your Google search...

would be motivating, but if your goal is too monumental you may end up giving up because it never seems close enough.

Small goals don't have to be a physical reward. I know that I don't like making phones calls, so what I like to do is to schedule my phone calling to occur at my favorite coffee shop drinking my favorite hipster-made concoction. Attaching my favorite drink to making phone calls gives instant gratification and helps me to look forward to the task. Find something positive to hook onto the tasks that you always try to skip.

Motivate yourself to adhere to your time block. If you get to the end of the week and you hit every item on your time block, what can you realistically do to treat yourself? Put $500 in a family vacation fund? A good bottle of bourbon?

No one knows how you tick better than you. Find rewards (big or small) that will work for you.

To tie everything together, when we are looking at time blocking and accountability, the most important thing is to take this seriously and to be accountable to YOUR-SELF.

 Yes, I just said that being accountable to yourself is the first step— but it can be good to structure rewards that can get your family excited and involved as well. If your 10-year-old is nagging you to meet your goals/make your calls so they can go on a trip, or to a fun family dinner, I promise you will be more likely to follow through; nobody wants to fail for their family. Your victories, small and large, will feel that much better when you get to celebrate them with those you love the most.

 If you do have children, motivate them to find you sales. Have them trained to inform you of any friends' parents who discuss moving. Train them to tell everyone that their parent is the best Realtor/lender/ widget sales person ever. What if they get you a sale? Pay up! Acceptable forms of payment may include but not limited to: fat stacks of Benjamins,[5] shopping trips, candy, video games, a high five and heartfelt thank you... you get the idea.

[5] Hundred dollar bills. Big stacks of them.

TANGIBLE ACTIVITY:

- Write or type the 3 most important tasks you need to accomplish. The easiest way to do this is to start every day with 3 things that you want to accomplish, and then to end the day with hopefully those items checked off, and hopefully a few extra. Write it down on your desk calendar, carry a date book, your phone calendar, an app or software, or a CRM system you already utilize. Where you document accomplishments isn't important, it just matters that you do it.

- Tomorrow, or before you repeat that task again, take a look at what you accomplished last time and evaluate yourself.

- Did you slack off? If so, you know you have to work that much harder next time. More importantly, analyze why you didn't hit your tasks with the gusto you should have, and adjust your strategy, or better control for outside forces that kept you from hitting your goal.

- Did you kick butt? You'll see those positive results because you wrote it down and can remember how to kick even more butt next time.

Always keep a record of what you accomplished and what activities did or did not lead to results. This will be invaluable in the long term for tracking what was successful and what was not. Over time you will be able to perfectly hone your strategies. The longer you do this, the more valuable the information becomes, and the more trends you will be able to spot. One trend that this has helped many in real estate plan better for is time off. After tracking your levels of business, and how different prospecting leads to new business, and on what timeline, you will have a better idea of the optimal vacation time due to when you have historically been the slowest.

Set goals of what you want to achieve and then work backwards to figure out how much time you need to time block to hit those goals. The longer you do this, and the more results-based data you track, the easier this will get.

 As you read this book, make sure to set time blocks in your calendar for the strategies that interest you. Once you time block for starting a strategy, set measurable goals and time to evaluate how they worked and what they led to.

FACEBOOK

———

I don't want to sound cliché by saying that Facebook is the latest and greatest thing for the real estate business, but right now it just might be. What's interesting is that when I started writing this in 2017, Facebook was exponentially sexier than where it ended in 2019 as I wrapped up this book. Between 2016 and now, millions of users have switched their primary social media focus to Instagram. Since Instagram is owned by Facebook and the data they have on customers is singularly owned, it is still pretty fair to say that Facebook as a company is a hugely beneficial tool for real estate professionals.

Still skeptical? Consider this: Facebook, more than any other social network is a data company. Real estate is about 2 things, relationships and data. If you can learn to leverage a data tool to strengthen your relationships you will increase your results.

Simply put, Facebook has been one of the single best tools for getting business that I have seen in the last decade. One of the reasons it has been so beneficial is that there are so many different ways to use it. It is no longer a social media site, it is a public square. But even better than a public square, where you can only hear what's going on, you can click any person and instantly get more information on them. This information is what makes Facebook such a powerful (and controversial) tool for businesses.

There are so many different ways to utilize Facebook for sales, most of which are completely free. Even the paid options offer benefits that traditional marketing has not offered to the same extent: think analytics (you can see how many people engaged with your content in real time), think the ability to constantly test and refine your content. If what you posted didn't deliver you the response you were hoping for, you can pivot or change course quickly—something that simply isn't possible with traditional forms of marketing like newspapers, TV ads, etc.

Even if you're not into social media in your personal life, there are still ways to use Facebook that can work for anyone, yes anyone. We will cover a variety of different strategies for Facebook, but first, let's talk about the medium itself.

Understanding The Medium

Facebook is friendly for sales people who are on the go; you do not need to be in your office or on a computer to benefit. You can literally "do" Facebook from any-where, right on your phone. More importantly, your customers can engage with you on the go, anytime as well. When you make it easier for people to engage with you, you are likely to get more engagements.

Facebook can help you to **"work smarter, not harder."**

For me, I like to go out to eat (A LOT), and sometimes eating at really good restau-rants means waiting for an hour or two. What you do when you are waiting at a restaurant (or waiting anywhere)? Waiting around often means staring off blankly into the abyss that is your cell phone. Whether your poison is browsing shopping sites or reading the trollish comments section on local news articles, we both know that these activities are unproductive. You know how important your time is, so spend it wisely. Two hours wasted is a huge deal, so why not open up the Facebook app and get marketing? Wasting time is a wasted opportunity—don't let the time slip through your fingers. A mobile marketing tool like Facebook is a great way to convert potentially wasted time into productive prospecting or client research.

Your Facebook Profile

When it comes to Facebook, think about your business strategy in terms of build-ing blocks. The first building block when it comes to social media is how complete your profile is. As with any marketing, you have to have the basic foundations set up before you can truly use it as a strategy for business. The mistake we most often see sales people making is that they start marketing before properly setting up their online profiles with correct info and settings. This can include privacy settings, profile photo, and all of the information that will be displayed to those who see you online.

If you plan to use Facebook for marketing (and you should), you need to make sure that your profile is at least public or semi-public. A private profile will hide your marketing from people that could be potential clients. If you are super concerned about privacy, then do not post anything that you feel is going to invade that privacy OR choose to set your privacy level on individual posts you create, but not on your profile in general.

After assessing your privacy settings, the next step revolves around how you title your job. For example, if you are a Realtor or a mortgage lender, make sure that the job title clearly and unequivocally explains what you do. It should say you are a sales person and clearly state the company you work for. I can't even express how silly it is when I see sales people that give themselves bloated titles like 'CEO of Real Estate Agency X' and 'Director of Realtor Services'. Please think long and hard before you come up with a job title that doesn't exactly explain what you do. You want people to understand what you do in the simplest terms possible. If the primary portion of your income comes from commissions, make sure your job title reflects the main product you sell. e.g. Realtor, Mortgage Loan Officer, etc. Keep in mind the majority of people out there are not the expert in what you do. It is not worth losing a sale because someone thought you were now in management and too big of a deal to work with them on their transaction.

There is a mortgage company that advertises heavily in my market where every single sales person in the company is the Vice President of something. A cool job title may be good for your ego and may even be great for picking up a date at the bar, but unless your ego is more important than actual sales, keep it simple.

What if you have more than one job? This is very common especially with new sales people who aren't ready to dive into full commission. If you fall into this boat, make sure that the one job or skill that pays you the highest commission or that you enjoy the most is front and center and does not get overshadowed. Some customers can be pretty wary if you have 17 different jobs, and your competitors will almost always look for potential weaknesses to relay back to a customer that you are both competing for. The great thing about Facebook is that YOU get to decide how the world sees you; leave as little open to interpretation as possible. Sure, your main income might come from one job, but if real estate is the vision for where you want your main income to come from in the future, show the world the reality that you want to be. Perception, after all, is reality.

Speaking of perception, keep in mind that everyone looks at things differently, so try to stay away from content that could offend potential customers/past clients (unless offensive shock and awe approaches are part of your brand and you can afford to lose people who don't prescribe to your style). If you wouldn't say it at work in front of your most sensitive coworker, you may not want to say it online.

It's all about priorities. If being your true self on Facebook is your utmost priority, that's okay, but if you would rather alleviate the risk of someone choosing not to work with you because of an old picture or a post about your favorite politician, then be cognizant of what you are typing or what you are allowing others to see publicly about you online.

TANGIBLE ACTIVITY:

Facebook Profile Checklist

☐ Is the name you use on Facebook one that friends will recognize & remember you by?
- Avoid nicknames.
- Put maiden name or name others might know you by in parentheses or hyphenate.

☐ Is the job title and current employer section filled out?
- Use the simplest job title possible.
- Put past jobs and employers in your profile to remind people how they know you, but not so many jobs that people will think you move around too much.

☐ Are you both easy to recognize and professional in your profile photo?
- Use a professional headshot whenever possible. If you are putting your kids/dog in your photo as well, make sure you are still the dominant part of the image and that you're showcasing a lifestyle that your friends and potential clients will identify with.

☐ Is your contact information filled out with the most up to date info?
- Only a fraction of Facebook users have their contact info filled out, yet it is one of the first places people search when looking for someone's contact info. If you are hoping to use Facebook for sales/marketing make sure it is as easy as possible for people to contact you.

☐ Is your profile set to public?
- Having your profile set to public is helpful, but check to ensure that the individual posts that you hope will serve a marketing purpose are also public as well. This can be a great way to filter who sees what at the post level rather than locking down your whole account.

Once you have a public Facebook profile that showcases you in the right light to your sought after audience, it's time to start marketing.

Facebook Marketing Strategies

Social media is like an online dinner party. Everyone has a different appetite, and invites a different audience. The strategies that we will outline next are meant to be a menu. Every item will be tangible, but there may be some that aren't your taste. When you go to a restaurant you can still have a great night without eating every item. Use the upcoming strategies to build your perfect experience. If something works, do more of it, adapt it, and improve. If something doesn't work, pay the check, remember the mistake, and move on.

Facebook Messaging Strategy

This strategy is really, really simple. You can use a social network to engage in networking with your existing network. The overall idea is that you are already connected on Facebook to people. Some you know really well, and others are people you took one class with 10 years ago. By using the messenger feature on Facebook you can engage, re-engage, and stay in front of an already lukewarm audience. If the concept of sending messages to random people you haven't talked to in a while makes you cringe, its because you don't think you have anything to say. Don't worry, we will cover solutions for this below.

Start with your friends list. Sort your list from A-Z.

Next, figure out how many people per day you want to message. Like we talked about earlier, make sure you hold yourself accountable for this and time block appropriately.

Click on someone you would like to reach out to and check out what they have been up to recently. Find something interesting to talk to them about. For instance, if you were going to look at my Facebook, you would see that I went on vacation recently. This is your conversation starter.

Shoot the person a message that asks them a question, or message them about one of their recent posts. When you engage with someone about something that they have recently posted about you are talking to them about something that you know they care about (or at least cared enough about to share with their friends on Facebook). Having a specific message about a topic they posted about increases their chance of responding exponentially. This is not a new concept! Dale Carnegie disuccses starting conversations this way in his 80+ year old sales classic "How To Win Friends and Influence People."[6]

Don't walk away from the conversation yet — this is where the magic happens. When you ask someone a question and they answer it, there is a huge chance that they will reciprocate by asking you a question back. Often times their follow up question will be a generic, "How's it going," or something similar. This type of open-ended question will give you a chance to guide the conversation where you want to take it. Rather than being salesy and annoying you can instead mention real estate or your desired topic in a positive way.

Example:
Me: Hey, John. I saw you guys went to went to Washington D.C. How was it? I'm thinking of going there soon as well.

John: Hey, Matt! You know I had a great time. You should definitely check out the museums, and the bars, preferably in reverse order lol. What have you been up to lately?

Me: Nice, that's awesome! We will definitely be checking out some museums (and a few drinks first will def make them more fun). I've been good. Work has been busy but fun, the real estate market has been hot, so I've been busy showing houses and writing offers etc.

Notice I did not actually try to sell them something, BUT I mentioned how great the market was doing and illustrated two tasks that an agent could perform for him or a referral. The point of this is not to make a sale right off the bat, but to remind people what you do in a positive way.

By not asking them a follow-up question (or changing the subject) after your response about real estate you are maintaining control over the conversation. This will often prompt the person you are chatting with to ask you a follow up about work or the real estate market. Keep in mind that like the weather, for the average person real estate is one of those universal topics that almost everyone is somewhat interested in, so this especially works to our advantage.

 [6] https://www.amazon.com/gp/product/0671027034/ref=dbs_a_def_rwt_bibl_vppi_i0

After a little casual banter about whatever you messaged your connection about, try to take it to the next level, not by offering them to do something real estate related, but by scheduling a coffee or drink to re-connect. Those who message you back and agree to a meeting, have thus shown that they like spending time with you and can be further cultivated for deep referrals and actual business.

Be genuine. By truly engaging and showing genuine interest in your friends' lives and chosen topic of conversation, you are guaranteed to see results and deepen relationships.

When you do this strategy 10 to 15 to 20 times a day, I'm not saying that those 10 to 20 contacts are all going to buy what you are selling. However, those 10 to 20 people are all interacting with another 20+ people on a daily basis. Although math and statistics are not my strongest skills, I would bet that this strategy will put the odds in your favor of picking up more referrals and even direct deals.

Same Tactic, Different Rationale

Although using the above strategy works great for the reasons we stated above, there are some fringe benefits as well. People who regularly use the messaging strategy often come to value this fringe benefit greatly. Agents started telling me about something extra that happens when you engage with people on Messenger due to Facebook's algorithm. Yes, even I shudder when I hear the word algorithm. It brings back bad flashbacks to 9th-grade math classes. Don't worry, you don't need to understand Facebook's entire algorithm to reap the benefits of the strategy. In fact, most algorithm's actions can barely be predicted by their creators in dynamic and actively changing situations like social media (think, did Cyberdyne Systems really think their coded Terminators would take over the world?[7])

Algorithm
[al-guh-rith-uh m] — noun

1. A process or set of rules to be followed in calculations or other problem-solving operations, especially by a computer.

---

[7] Really cool Terminator movie reference.

Bad sci-fi and math references aside, for now, let's just focus on one aspect of Facebook's algorithm that adds some extra value to those who use the messaging strategy. When you message someone on Facebook, the algorithm makes a little note that you are more interested in that person and they are more interested in you. After a few messages back and forth you are likely to both start seeing more of each other's posts in your news feeds. This is good because if you're using Facebook for marketing, these rekindled relationships who may not be recently familiar with you professionally now have a higher chance of getting exposed to you and your brand.

To recap, using the Facebook message strategy you can literally have a win-win situation wherein the best case scenarios you set appointments and get referrals, and at the very least you get more free publicity on the other Facebook posts you were already planning to do. In fact, if you start to notice the engagement dropping on your normal posts, the messaging strategy could be a good way to increase your likes, comments and overall viewership.

Recent work with Instagram, which is owned by Facebook, also suggests that their algorithm operates in a similar way. Those who you direct message back and forth are also more likely to see your posts in their feed.[8]

Avoid Bad Advice From People Who "Don't Get It" — Stay Authentic

As with any good marketing idea, lazy sales people, their coaches, brokers, and managers have found ways to slowly ruin the strategy. I was at a real estate marketing presentation where the guy on stage pitched "a brilliant script for prospecting with Facebook." The coach gave a handout, which was actually titled: "AN EXACT SCRIPT TO FOLLOW."

My head almost exploded. The script he passed out was three paragraphs that he undoubtedly copied from a script meant for email marketing from 10 years ago. There was nothing personal about the script, and it was all about the sender. It even had a signature/sign off at the end. I was in agony!

[8] https://buffer.com/library/instagram-feed-algorithm

Now think for a moment... what would you do if you received a three-paragraph message that was not only unsolicited, but was also trying to sell you something without even trying to pretend to engage you? Maybe call me pretty before you try to take me home? I can honestly say that if someone sent me a 3 paragraph long message I would ignore it 100 percent of the time. **Be real to people on social media, and have fun with it.**

The more fun you have with a strategy, the more you will do it anyways. Find an aspect of Facebook or Instagram that you enjoy and use it to authentically connect with others. Regardless of which social site is the hot one of the moment, if you look at social media in this lens you will be equipped to succeed in any environment.

Take The Next Steps

Here is the caveat, if you are going to use the Facebook messaging strategy, then you need to keep checking back. You won't get responses right away all the time. You have to check in. Time block to check in after you send out a batch of messages. Then you can check in on any responses and answer in the ways we discussed that will take your conversations to the next level.

Facebook Messenger is one of the best places where you can take a relationship from online to real life. In person meetings and hangouts will help you to develop these relationships to the next level. Whether your first step is a phone call, text, or something else, it is important to treat new (or newly engaged) Facebook social media relationships like a seed. Work on them often, and they will grow.

I have worked with both agents and lenders who use this strategy religiously and experience real results from it. Some of the agents used it to generate 25+ deals in their first year. These are not mega-rich real estate agents with a huge marketing budget, these are people who time blocked and turned their existing Facebook network into a referral machine.

Personal Pages VS. Business Pages

Everything that we discussed above for Facebook can be done at no cost to you. It can also all be accomplished using your personal Facebook profile without having to have a business page. Do you need a business page? If you only plan to do the above things, and you have nothing to hide in your personal life, then no! However, if you hope to use Facebook to also do paid advertising, than you do need a business page.

The reason I don't think that every person needs a business page is that it can become redundant. Try to answer the questions: Who will like my business page who doesn't already like my personal page? How will I get people to like my business page? If your plan to grow your business page is to invite people who already like your personal page, what's the point? Is the content you post going to be so radically different? Are you comfortable spending money to reach the same people you could have already reached for free? For those users who want to keep their personal page 100% personal and not use it at all for marketing, a business page can be a great option, but the number of people you reach, and the number of people who engage with you will not be as large, unless you pay to boost or promote your content.

FACEBOOK — PAID ADVERTISING

Disclaimer

Rules for advertising are constantly changing. In March of 2019, the Department of Housing and Urban Development charged Facebook with violating the Fair Housing Act,[9] aand also went after numerous lenders and real estate agencies (agents) for using Facebook's advertising platform to allegedly discriminate — by limiting the housing choices shown to some users. As of May 2019, Facebook has given the label of "special category" to ads that pertain to real estate, housing, lending, credit, employment and a few others. Advertisers will now check a box when they go to create an ad that will tell facebook if your ad fits into one of those categories. For now, this is ad based and not account based. Facebook has already deleted many targeting options (that real estate professionals were heavily using) for those who check the special category box from their platform. Facebook did however leave many options for interest-based targeting which for now are fine to use and are still great opportunities. At the time of this writing it is still also unclear whether a real estate agent or lender doing an ad that promotes their brand or culture can still use the demographic targeting options or not. From the testing that I have done, it seems like it works half the time – and the other half of the time Facebook's algorithm lets your ad run for a few days and then disapproves it. Once disapproved you can submit your ad for review and try to make the case that your ad simply advertises a different facet of your company and doesn't fall into a special category. From what we can see, this again works sometimes, but not always.

I still wanted to include information on Facebook advertising in this book because it is still a viable option that has a positive ROI, but as with any marketing it may be a good idea to consult with your broker, attorney or in house compliance team before getting started. A best practice to follow to play it safe would be to ensure that you aren't targeting or excluding people from seeing all of your ads based on protected class demographic information such as age, sex, race and a few others.

Don't want to hear about my interpretation of how to use Facebook for advertising in real estate or lending? Here is the most updated information we have right from FB itself as of October 2019.

Choosing a Special Ad Category: If you're based in or targeting the U.S. and are creating a campaign that includes ads that offer credit, employment or housing opportunities, you must choose the category that best describes your ads. These are special categories for which audience selection tools are limited to help protect people on Facebook from unlawful discrimination. Choosing the correct category for your campaign is an important part of following Facebook's advertising policies. These special categories include, but are not limited to ads that offer credit, housing or employment opportunities.

Special Ad Categories
- *Credit Opportunity: Ads that promote or directly link to a credit opportunity, including but not limited to credit card offers, auto loans, personal or business loan services, mortgage loans and long-term financing. This also includes brand ads for credit cards, regardless of a specific offer.*

[9] https://www.housingwire.com/articles/48484-hud-still-pursuing-facebook-for-allowing-housing-discrimination-despite-ad-changes

- *Employment Opportunity: Ads that promote or directly link to an employment opportunity, including but not limited to part- or full-time jobs, internships or professional certification programs. Related ads that fall within this category include promotions for job boards or fairs, aggregation services or ads detailing perks a company may provide, regardless of a specific job offer.*

- *Housing Opportunity or Related Service: Ads that promote or directly link to a housing opportunity or related service, including but not limited to listings for the sale or rental of a home or apartment, homeowners insurance, mortgage insurance, mortgage loans, housing repairs and home equity or appraisal services. This does not include ads designed to educate consumers or housing providers about their rights and responsibilities under fair housing laws. You can include the Equal Opportunity Housing logo and slogan to help differentiate your ads as non-discriminatory.*

This is not a comprehensive list of examples and does not constitute legal advice.

Audience selection tools for Special Ad Categories: Certain targeting options are not available for ads in special categories; this includes Lookalike Audiences. However, to help you reach people who may be interested in your ad, you can create a Special Ad Audience, which will create an audience based on similarities in online behavior and activity but that does not use certain categories, including age, gender, ZIP code or other similar categories.
Note: Certain targeting options such as Special Ad Audience and Custom Audience may only be available via Ads Manager.

We encourage you to broaden — not restrict — your audience. Our targeting options, like all audience selection tools on Facebook, must be used in ways that are inclusive and not discriminatory.

The other main reason I am writing this caveat is to inform you that if you are using a 3rd party advertising agency or person to run your Facebook ads, it might be wise to check with them to see who is being targeted and or excluded, and then check with your broker, manager, or compliance team to ensure you are not in violation.

Rules governing these sorts of things, and other traditional marketing as well, are very fluid; however, please take all of the advice in the following sections with a grain of salt, and ensure that you only advertise in ways that you feel are ethically responsible – and practical for your goals and budget.

Already using Facebook ads and not sure if they are compliant? Don't worry. There are self-testing rules that urge all advertisers to test their own ads for targeting violations that may be exclusionary, if you find a mistake and correct it, then document that you fixed it on your own; the correction of the violation is considered privileged and doesn't open you up to liability as long as it is done right. For more information on this check out the footnote link below.[10]

Getting Started

People ask me all the time about where they should be spending their advertising dollars and how they should be getting the word out about their product or their service. Oftentimes one of the easiest and cheapest ways to do marketing, if you really want to target an audience with a specific set of interests, is Facebook advertising (also includes Instagram ads, because they run on the same platform). There are two types of paid Facebook advertising: boosted posts, and ad campaigns. The main difference is that boosted posts can be done right from your business page on a per post basis, and an ad campaign won't actually show up as content on your business page but will show up in the news feeds of the people you are targeting. Boosted posts are great when you are on the go and want to advertise something that is a one-time event like an open house or a temporary drop in interest rates. Ads Manager campaigns are better when you want your content to be more of an ongoing strategy. The main benefit of doing a campaign through the Ads Manager is that Facebook learns and improves how and to whom it displays your ads over time. In essence, it allows Facebook to get smarter and helps your ads to perform better.

Even if you aren't super comfortable with social media, and it seems daunting, keep reading. We break it down to make it as easy as possible, so you can achieve tangible results.

What I love about Facebook is that it's advertising platform has a detailed targeting portfolio. There are literally hundreds of demographic and interest based choices that you can select when you are choosing who you want to see your ad.

Just a few Facebook ad targeting examples that are pertinent to real estate:

- City – *If it's a "special category" ad, you must select a radius of at least 15 miles around a given city or address, I recommend address.*
- Age – *Although you CAN NOT target specific ages anymore for special category ads you CAN target based on interests that you think young people would have. Examples include First Time Home Buyers, Renting, Entry Level Job, First Job, Starter Home.*
- Apartments, Apartment Guide, Apartment List
- Architecture & Design
- Broker

- Cash Out Refinancing
- Condominiums
- Cottage
- Creative Real Estate Investing
- Credit
- Credit Karma, Credit Sesame
- Credit Limit
- Custom Home
- Duplex
- Estate Agent
- FHA Insured Loan
- First Time Buyer
- First Time Buyer Grant
- Fixer Upper
- Floor Plan
- For Sale By Owner
- Gated Community
- Home Construction
- Home Equity Loan
- HELOC
- Home Improvement
- Home Insurance
- Homes.com
- House Hunting
- Interest Rate
- Interior Design
- Land and Houses
- Landlord
- Loan Officer
- Loan
- Luxury Real Estate
- Manufactured Housing
- Mobile Home
- Modern Architecture
- Mortgage Broker
- Mortgage Insurance
- Mortgage Loans
- Moving Company
- Multiple Listing Service
- Owner Occupier
- Penthouse Apartment
- Prequalification
- Prefabricated Home
- Property Finder
- Real Estate Agent Directory
- Real Estate
- Real Estate Appraisal
- Real Estate Broker
- Real Estate Development
- Real Estate Investing
- Real Estate License
- Realtor.com, Zillow, Trulia
- Refinancing
- Remortgage
- Renovation
- Rent To Own, Rent.com, Renting
- Single Family Detached Home
- Starter Home
- Townhouse

Regardless of which targeting options you choose, make your goal to get your ad in front of the smallest, most narrow and specific group of people for whom your ad would be relevant and interesting. Not every ad or every Facebook post you do should have the same targeting specs or overall audience. For example, if you want to run a Facebook Ad for an open house, your goal is to target people who are likely to come to that specific open house.

With so many targeting options to choose from many real estate professionals and would be marketers get paralyzed trying to select them and give up on the strategy right here. Choosing the right targeting options is all about a little creative thinking, relative to the people who have been your customers in the past, or who you would like them to be in the future. In the coming section, we will discuss the "why" behind some of the more popular targeting options.

Targeting Options: Age & Income

Although you can no longer target ages specifically for special category based ads, you can still get creative and target the interests that people in your desired age ranges are likely to have. Take a moment and look through the list on the previous pages to think about which options might help you market a relatively inexpensive small home. Similarly which interests would you use if you were advertising a million dollar listing? Options like starter home, first time home buyer, renter and many others may be great options for getting closer to your desired age group, while options like philanthropy, luxury real estate and home construction may be better options for advertising your higher end promotions.

Targeting Options: Geographic

The fastest way to lose money on Facebook is to target too large of a geographic area. In contrast, the easiest way to make an impact and ensure that a large percentage of your desired population sees your ad is to target the smallest and most targeted area you can. For ads that fall under the "special category" rule – your geographic choices include the city you want to target plus 15 miles and zip code targeting is no longer an option. Even if your ad doesn't fall into the special category rules one thing to watch out for is that when you type an area in, Facebook's ad manager will automatically prompt you to target people within 10-25 miles of that selection. This is almost never a good idea because it can drain your budget fast, especially if you are targeting a very populated area. On the other hand, if you live in a very rural area with sparse population numbers using the +10 or even +25 mile options can be a time-saver.

One time, a Realtor marketing a lake home told me he tried to spend $200 targeting people in Chicago. He typed in Chicago and it added +25 miles. His $200 was spent in minutes. Be specific when possible.

When you are running an ad for an open house or marketing a specific property, try using targeting that focuses on that area or a similar area. For instance, if there are two or three high-end areas in your market and you have a high-end home that sold, advertising the sale in both of those areas might be a good strategy. However, if your budget only allows you to target one of those areas, then choose the one where the home is physically located.

Targeting Options: Gender

Special category ads are NOT allowed to target by gender; however, since other ads are, we will use the below section to describe the logic behind gender and targeting.

99% of the time the ads I create target both men and women. Occasionally though, you will have content to advertise that may be better geared towards one or the other. These are often great opportunities to have some fun and to make your ads more relevant by making them more specific. For instance, if the house you are featuring in an ad has a urinal, and you want to really get some shares/publicity, narrowing your audience to men only, and featuring the urinal in your ad creative, could be a great strategy. This type of post would have a certain "shareable" value which will thus help your ad get in front of more eyeballs for less money. Using this same logic, a goal for almost any social media campaign is for it to go viral.

Going viral cannot be planned or guaranteed; however, a savvy advertiser can increase their chances of content going viral by promoting/targeting their content initially to a narrow niche audience most likely to react and engage with it. Even if you are following the rules and can't target gender specifically, simply using imagery in your ads that will appeal to your ideal target is a step in the right direction towards going more viral. (Author's note: my wife said we aren't allowed to have a urinal in the house.)

Targeting Options: Language

If the house you are marketing is in a very culturally diverse neighborhood, then it might be wise to target languages that make the most sense for your population. In fact, since almost all real estate ads in the US are in English, someone seeing an ad in their first language may make it stand out more.

This doesn't mean that your actual ad should say, "Hey Spanish speaking people" because that would be discriminatory. But in the targeting options, you can target any language you want to. Similarly, you could even run two separate ads to the same house, one in English and one in Spanish. In each of the targeting settings, you could target the English ad to English speakers and the Spanish ad to Spanish speakers.

Targeting Options: Relationship Status

Special category ads are NOT allowed to target by relationship status; however, since other ads are, we will use the below section to describe the logic behind relationship status targeting.

Many agents and lenders have had success running ads to engaged people or those in a new relationship. The logic here is that home ownership often starts right before or after a wedding. Although this is probably less true now than 20 years ago, this logic can still get you closer to a likely home buyer when placing online ads.

Facebook even has options to target based on how long people have been in these life stages. You can choose to target only newlyweds or people who have been engaged for a long or short time. Again, by starting with narrow targeting and testing to see which combinations yield you the best results you can continually tune your strategy.

Be Narrow, But Not Too Narrow

Targeting to a narrow group will help you to get the biggest bang for your buck, but if you narrow down your audience too small you could end up targeting nobody at all. A good comparison in the real world is online dating. Let's say you have a type, a very specific type. You are trying to find all single, Asian, men who live within one mile of your zip code who went to Michigan State University, who are interested in real estate investing who speak Spanish as their first language. Sure, these are all parameters you could target in your search, but the likelihood that this person exists is very low. If your target is too small, nobody will see your ad, but too broad of an audience and your budget will disappear quickly to an uninterested audience. Find a good middle ground.

Lucky for you, Facebook doesn't want you to fail. When you are setting your targets, you will see an indicator on the right-hand side of the screen showing you both how many people fit your targeting parameters, and a recommended budget to use. Try to find audiences over 1,000 people for best results. Unless your budget is huge, also try to stay below 250,000. If you target a large group with a small budget, your ad will get lost in the shuffle and is not likely to work.

Similar Audience Targeting: Reaching "Lookalike" Audiences

If you have never done Facebook marketing before, don't start here. This is a targeting method that is recommended for you to try only after you have figured out and tested some of the above targeting methods. The reason is that you need to build an audience that you know is accurate and that begins to deliver you results before you try to replicate it. With similar audience targeting, Facebook allows the advertiser to choose an existing audience they are targeting and generate a "lookalike" audience of people with similar characteristics.

This is the kind of creative targeting that big companies (and political campaigns) are using, and that real estate industry marketers charge large amounts to help you perform. That being said, it can be done on a relatively low budget (as little as $5/day), and after some testing, you could be up and running within a week or less.

In addition to reaching audiences that are similar to your existing targeting parameters, you can also upload lists of your past clients' names/emails, and if your list is big enough, Facebook can use that list to generate a list of other users with similar interests. In theory, these people share characteristics with those people who already chose to work with you, they may even be friends or friends of your friends. This type of targeting is thus a good way of getting you in front of an audience that is significantly more likely to work with, or need you.

A small caveat for those trying similar audience targeting (and who want to use a custom list upload to create the initial audience) is that the list you upload to get started has to be big enough for Facebook to use to spot trends. This usually means at least 100 people. However, we have seen the greatest success when the initial list uploaded is at least 5,000 users. Although this number may seem impossible to reach for some agents, it is an especially exciting idea if you have been purchasing online leads for years. Many of you may have upwards of 10,000 leads in your Zillow or another marketing platform, why not use that data to build a better list of targets.

Facebook Retargeting

If you have had some degree of practice with Facebook marketing, either through using specific targeting or using the messaging strategy, and you are ready for something else that will help you to stand out, try retargeting.

Retargeting
(also known as Remarketing)

1. A form of online advertising that can help you track people who visit your website (and other digital properties) and then send ads to them to stay in top of mind.

Now, this may sound confusing, technical, and a bit crazy, but let me explain what Facebook Retargeting is. For example, say you are searching for a vacation online. You visit a travel website and browse some hotels. If the website has retargeting code on it, it will track your cookies and then serve up related travel ads to you in the weeks that follow. After reading that example I challenge you to search for anything travel related for even five minutes. I would almost guarantee that at least 75% of the sites you visit begin to track and retarget ads to you within the next week. A website tracked your information and is now re-serving you ads with relevant content. You don't have to be a big company to do this. Anyone can do this, and I've done this successfully with a budget as small as $5 a day. If you do choose to do this, the best practice is to update the privacy policy on your website to let people know you may be retargeting them.

I personally love this type of marketing for myself and my clients because it accomplishes two main goals. First, it gets me a second chance in front of website visitors who might not have converted into leads. Second, it gives me a way to stay top of mind to people who are already at least a little bit familiar with my brand.

This can be one of the highest return on investment/awareness pieces of advertising you can do, will make you stand out from many of your local competitors, and best of all should take you less than 30 minutes to initially set up.

If you go into Facebook's audience manager (only available if you already have a business page, and have done at least one boosted post or paid ad) you can create something called a pixel. The pixel that you create will be embedded on your website. It's a little snippet of code and super easy to install if you have a website that is easy to make changes on. Alternatively, if you have a website but aren't super tech savvy, you can likely Google how to do it, or ask someone in your office for help.

Once you take the pixel code from the audience manager on Facebook and plug it into your website, your site will begin tracking every click that comes to your site based on the visitor's browser cookies. Then, Facebook is going to start talking behind the scenes with your website. If that same person who was on your website goes on Facebook (or Instagram if you choose), Facebook will add them to your retargeting list, giving you the ability to send ads to these people.

Once you have more than a couple hundred people on your retargeting list, you then can create an ad that targets people whose data was captured by the pixel. Through the power of retargeting, whatever ad you design will be presented in front of anyone who went to your website who then also goes on Facebook.

The reason I like this form of marketing is that it is one step ahead of targeting random people who are less likely to react to your message. I always encourage people to start their marketing in areas where they will have the highest probability of success. Any marketing that gets and keeps you in front of people who already even vaguely familiar with you is a win. Facebook retargeting is an inexpensive and easy way to stay top of mind, and to get a second chance in front of people who went to your site but left.

PRO TIP: *You can create different retargeting ads for people who completed different actions on your website or who visited different pages. For example, you could create separate ads for people who used your site to look at homes in one city vs. another and then retarget ads to each user that match their home buying budget and past page views on your site. The bigger your website and the more traffic you get, the more retargeting options you will have.*

The Logic Behind Your Targeting Choices And A Short Disclaimer

It is important to choose the right targeting demographics, but make sure to check with your broker/manager or your state's legal hotline if you aren't sure the ways in which you are or aren't allowed to target from a fair housing rules perspective. In some people's eyes, choosing your targeting parameters can be a touchy subject because, by definition, targeting one group means you are not targeting another — not to mention that Facebook lets you exclude entire groups for non-special category ads. The opinions in this book do not advocate for discrimination, but rather that you choose your ad targeting and placement options in a way that ensures you are able to reach your ideal audience for your ideal budget.

Pick Your Target, Then Set Goals

Facebook is good for many things, but it is a good practice to figure out what you want to get out of Facebook's ads before you start paying for them. Many sales people have very different goals and purposes for using, or wanting to use, Facebook advertising. Some agents aren't even looking for results, they simply want to be able to honestly tell potential buyers and sellers that they market on Facebook to give themselves an edge over the next agent who might not mention it. It is absolutely okay if this is your goal, but if so, your budget can be small.

Others have a goal of getting more branding and awareness behind themselves, a listing, or even an event they are hosting. For branding and awareness-based goals, make sure to figure out how many times you want your target market to see your ads. After narrowing down your audience this data will help you to set the correct budget.

Another common objective is to get more views/exposure on a video. This could be a video about you, your team, or even about a listing. If video views are your goal, you can actually choose it as an objective when you go to set up your ads through the Ads Manager. Facebook will then show your ads more frequently to those in your target likely to watch the videos, and who ostensibly are on an internet connection fast enough for them to load.

The most common goal that we usually hear, is to get leads. Most commonly, leads from the general public, or people that don't know you. This is often both the hardest and the easiest goal to accomplish. Generating leads, in general, is fairly easy, while generating high quality leads that are likely to turn into closed deals in a short time frame is difficult and requires hard work, planning and follow up.

For those chasing this goal, first consider where you are sending traffic to — do people who click on your ad end up on your website? If so, is your website optimized to capture leads? In essence, in order to have an ad on social media that works, you need to have a creative advertisement that prompts viewers to either enter their information onto a form on Facebook or on a website (a website that will then send you that lead information). In order to not flush your money down the drain, it is important to ensure that your website has something appealing on it that will convince customers who click your Facebook ad to follow through and enter their information. Typically, most websites/landing pages will offer visitors something in exchange for their information. A free guide, a list of homes, a discount, an immediate phone call, etc.

If your website and or landing page is optimized to capture leads (with an appealing message or offer that matches your ad content) you can continue on in Facebook's Ads Manager and move to the next step which is setting up conversion tracking. If it isn't, skip to the next chapter.

Facebook defines a conversion[11] as:

An action that a person takes on your website such as checking out, registering, adding an item to the shopping cart, or viewing a particular page. Virtually any page on your website can represent a conversion, and you can create and add the Face-book pixel code on any page of your website.

Facebook allows you to place a line of code called a pixel from Facebook onto your websites for the purpose of tracking the actions that your customers take after clicking on your ad. The reason savvy advertisers should do this is because it will help you to better track exactly which clicks led to which results. With this data in hand you can say with certainty how many leads you received from your Facebook ad and which ad creative, or even which of your targeting parameters worked best, and netted you leads for the lowest cost (at hopefully the highest quality).

Don't Have A Landing Page Or Website To Send Your Ad Traffic To?

If your goal is to capture leads, but you don't have a website with a good lead capture system that relates to the offer in your ads, you need to either re-evaluate your goals, or look to outside tools to build an easy to navigate landing page on your website that you can direct traffic to. Similarly, there are a lot of companies out there where you can, in essence, rent landing pages which are already geared towards real estate. For an example of a company that has specific pre-made land-ing pages geared towards real estate and lending, check out Instapage.[12]

An alternative option to sending traffic from your ads away to a landing page on a website would be to use Facebook Lead Ads, which keeps users on Facebook the entire time and simply pops up with a box asking for their name and email address. The simplicity here is that especially on for users on their cell phones it might be more convenient for them to quickly type their name and info in to get what they want vs. leaving the Facebook app and going to your website.

This can be a great option for those without a site of their own and the ability to add custom pages. It just depends on what your what your objective is. If you want to collect information like a user's name and their email, this might be a great option. One thing to watch out for here is quality. Often times the contact info people use

[11] Conversion Definition https://www.facebook.com/business/help/296943643749016
[12] https://instapage.com/lp/real-estate-landing-pages

on Facebook that would come to you in a lead ad could be the email address that they first used to sign up for Facebook with, or their preferred junk email address. Sure, the same email address could get used on a landing page, but the goal is that if your offer is cool and unique enough people will give you better contact information. Another benefit from getting them off of Facebook and onto your website is that you are bringing them to a place where they can get a real feel for your brand. On your website, you control the user experience. Similarly, if you are using a tracking pixel on your website, once someone is on your website you can stay in front of them by re-targeting other ads back to them.

Setting A Budget

The ideas in this chapter are useful for planning budgets for any marketing campaigns, not just Facebook. The content relates more to how to plan your spending based on possible ROT.

One of the biggest questions I get when people ask about Facebook advertising is how much they need to spend. Social media advertising doesn't have to be expensive, but every penny you spend should be purposeful. Think about it this way, every penny you spend is going to get you in front of a certain amount of people. What I usually recommend is starting small just to test out your content/messaging and to get more comfortable with it. If you can spend $10 a day and generate two leads a day, then you should be able to multiply your budget in hopes to receive the same ratio of leads per dollar you spend.

In terms of real estate, you also have to consider your life and needs. For example, if you are spending a hundred dollars a day on ads, that is going to add up to $3,000 a month, let's say that gets you 100 leads. 100 leads sounds like a lot, but how many of those are likely to convert into a sale? What does your history show? What other expenses will you incur working these leads? Will you close these leads at a full commission or will you refer them to someone on your team on a split commission model? How much time will you have to put into working them? How much is your time worth? Ask yourself these questions and figure out your true return on investment. Test this out and make sure that the budget you are setting makes sense for your possible return.

The above are also questions that will be helpful for you to ask yourself once you are already advertising and getting some measurable results. From results, I have seen from agents and lenders the average number of leads that turn into sales (from targeted marketing on sources like Facebook, Google, and Zillow) is somewhere around 4% for an average agent and 8% for a more experienced agent/team. Additionally, it can take anywhere from 2-12 months for these leads to translate into closed sales. This means that if 100 leads costs you $3,000 and you end up closing 6 deals (in the middle between 4-8%) you can multiply by the deal sizes and then by your commission to find out if it is worth it. For most sales people, the numbers do make sense, and you will make a profit. The big reason you need to think about how your budget fits into your overall strategy is that closing those 100 leads may also incur other expenses such as your time, broker fees, CRM fees, and others.

The amount of money you decide to spend should also reflect how many people are in your audience, the number of times you want each person to see your ad, and the number of days you want your ad to run. The more total eyeballs you want on your ad, the more you will need to budget. Facebook does have multiple types of budgets you can set. You can do an ad and boost it for a set amount of money for a set amount of time. You can also set a daily budget but tell Facebook to run your ad indefinitely until you turn it off. Finally, you can give Facebook a total dollar amount and set it as a lifetime budget such that once the money runs out your ad will stop.

Using Facebook Targeting For Home Value Leads

One of the things many Realtors have been doing for the last couple of years is using Facebook ads to target consumers, offering to get them a value of what their home might be worth. Of note, many lenders use a similar strategy offering people an idea of their home value in order to let them see how much equity they may have, to explore refinance options, or to best plan for an upcoming move. Although this is by no means a new strategy, it works because it offers something intriguing that almost all homeowners are always curious about. After all, home is one of the biggest assets that most humans will ever have.

Especially for people under 40, homes are often going to be worth more than their 401k. Human curiosity to know what this biggest asset might be worth creates the perfect set of circumstances that allows for these home value ads to be successful. If you're in a good economy, giving someone a home value that's higher than they expected can be a great way to get them to think about selling their home — hopefully with you.

Taking what you have learned about Facebook targeting, and now understanding that consumers like to know their home values, what kind of ads can we create? An easy ad to run is one is that is targeted to people on Facebook who live in a certain city or zip code, who make up a demographic that interests you, and to offer them a "Click Here" to find out what their home is worth.

The biggest piece of advice I can offer regarding home value ads is to make your ad copy and image as specific to the area you are targeting as possible. Many agents and marketers will use generic stock photos and will target huge areas. This leaves you with ads that are simply not relevant or proximate to any one person. Additionally, since consumers have already been seeing these ads for years, try to figure out a way to make your ads stand out.

Example:
As we just discussed, being more specific is key. I, for example, live in an area called Grand Rapids. People use the term Grand Rapids to refer to the whole region, even though only a portion of people actually own homes in the City of Grand Rapids. Thus targeting the name Grand Rapids, and using only the actual city in my geographic targeting is not likely to get me many leads. If I wanted to target my home value ads to an area in Grand Rapids, I would choose a specific zip code and try to find an area in my city that has a unique name. This could be a smaller subset of the city or a large neighborhood that has a unique identity. It can even include marketing to a smaller city that is close by. Then I could do a separate ad group for each city that makes up the collective "Grand Rapids" but in each ad set I could mention the more specific area it targets to better relate to users in those areas.

Another way to improve and hone this strategy is to make sure that the images used in your ad matches the actual area named in the copy. There's nothing worse than when I see a Facebook ad showing some Realtor or home in Michigan but the house in the ad looks like some Beverly Hills mansion. Tricking someone into clicking on your ad will only cost you extra money, waste their time, and lower your overall amount of quality leads.

Make sure you have a photo that makes sense to your audience and make sure there's some kind of pop of color. Ad images that are colorful are going to stand out a little bit more when people are scrolling through all of the other images and updates in their newsfeed. If you are creating your ad in the ads manager, it can also be wise to use multiple images. Facebook will allow you to create an ad with up to 6 different images. Facebook will then rotate them (with the same ad copy), and every week (or whenever you choose) you can go in and delete the image that performed worst and try something new in its place. Every time you delete something and put something in its place, make notes about what has worked and what hasn't so you don't repeat your failed attempts. This type of weekly testing can help to ensure that your marketing is always improving.

As with the ads we discussed above, the most important thing is home value ads only work well if you have a website/landing page that can capture someone's information and deliver a home value, sometimes referred to as a Competitive Market Analysis (CMA) or an Automated Valuation Model (AVM). If you want to begin doing home value ads and need a landing page that can deliver one to a customer, below are some places to start:

1. If you are with a major brokerage, check to see if your current website has an option for this. Many of the national brokerages provide tools such as Cloud CMA in the agent's website, or as a separate tool.

2. Check to see if your current brokerage or any of your affiliations gives you access to software or a CRM system that can do this. Top Producer, Kunversion, and a few other CRM's have at different times offered landing pages for home values, or let you create them.

3. Buy a tool that will give values. There are websites that agents and even lenders can buy (or lease) that offer CMA's or AVM's with prices starting as low as $50/month for single page websites that let visitors type in an address in exchange for a quick automated value estimate that gets sent to their email and to yours.

Even if your company doesn't already offer you a tool for this, and you don't have the budget for new software, you still have options.

The poor man's way to do home value ads without fancy software and also the least techy way to do this is to create a page on your website with a form that says "Enter your information for free home value, and I'll email it to you in the next 24 hours." This can cost you nothing and still get you some leads. That being said, it is a less preferential than a system where the potential customer receives an instant value and a note saying you will follow up and give more detailed information. If you opt to go this route, it can often help to include information on why waiting 24 hours will allow you to provide them with a more detailed estimate than an instant one. In all things marketing, it pays to explain your value.

A common thing to note is that with these kinds of leads, people will fill in their address for the home they want a value on, but then when you ask them for more information, they often give up without completing your form/request. These are people who figured out that they don't want a Realtor/lender calling them 100 million times. For these people, you at least captured their address which can become a possible doorknocking lead, or you can send them a letter with an offer of next steps to take. Overall, if you have an address, make sure you do something with it. If someone entered an address but stopped there, you at least know they have some level of curiosity. These are just a couple of things to think about if you are interested in running home value ads on social media. With these types of ads you do have to spend some money; however, my team used this strategy last year to generate sales people an average of 2 seller leads for $10, thus an average cost of $5 per lead. The quality varied; however, all agents we worked with did report closing deals with at least 10% of the total leads they received.

USING FACEBOOK FOR FREE

Getting More Business From Facebook Without Posting, Running Ads, OR Spending Money

The Power Of The Almighty Database

Explode Your Growth

Getting More Business From Facebook Without Posting, Running Ads, OR Spending Money

You have already learned how to use Facebook for lead generation. Now, I'm going to give you the easiest way to start getting more business on Facebook from people you are already connected to. This will help not only with direct lead generation but also with collecting more business intelligence and reconnaissance on potential clients.

The tactic we are about to cover is something that any person in any sales based position should be doing but probably isn't because it sounds time consuming. The tactic is to use Facebook like your Rolodex.[13] If you are in the business of collecting relationships, there is no better tool than social media for clicking "add friend" once you meet someone new in order to save and grow that relationship. If you have been doing this for years like I have, there is a good chance you have a pretty big list of connections, even if you aren't doing anything with it. Most of us have at least 500 friends on Facebook, 30% of whom or more likely have contact information displayed in their about section. If you have 500 friends and you can pull 30% of their information, that is an extra 150 people to add to your database for deeper prospecting. Consider the value of a phone number, email, or address, compared to making cold calls to people who don't even know you. People who you already have some familiarity with are much better sources for marketing because you have at least some trust built with them already.

TANGIBLE ACTIVITY:

1. Login to your Facebook and click on your friends list.

3. Sort your friends in alphabetical order.

4. Check out every person, or a set number of people for the day.

5. Look at their contact info.

6. See what is listed (e.g. Name, Birthdate, Address, Spouse, whatever)

7. Add necessary pieces to your spreadsheet/database/CRM

---

[13] Rolodex- A medieval address book on wheels. Rather than type in a name or ask Siri for a number or address users would hand write information in, and then sort with their thumbs by process of alphabetical order.

All of the items above are valuable pieces of information for marketers. Even if many of these people are already in your CRM database with contact info, adding anniversaries and interests can take your marketing game to the next level. I especially like to have personal information and notes so that when I do reach out, I can use these tidbits as icebreakers. For example, look someone up on Facebook before your prospecting call to find a conversation starter/icebreaker. Simply remembering the name of your prospect's child or pet can lower the chances of an immediate hang up, and if you are lucky, make them want to actually do business with you. People like people who show interest in them.

Whether you are using an expensive and robust CRM like SalesForce or a simple Excel spreadsheet, the more information you have, the more fuel you will have in your prospecting and appointment conversion efforts.

The Power Of The Almighty Database

Before we discuss the almighty database, let's discuss what a database is and what it's not. Put in basic terms, a databse is an organized system that is used to store data on people you hope to or already have done business with. A database is not simply your sphere of influence (SOI), because having an SOI doesn't necessarily mean that it is typed out or in any kind of organized system that you can easily draw on for marketing. I meet with sales people all the time who tell me they have a database, but when I ask them where it is stored they tell me that it is really just their cell phone contact list and email contact list. This may be considered your sphere of influence, but it is not a database because the data inside it cannot be easily called upon when it is time to start marketing. Although many sales people get lucky and can close a good number of deals off incoming referrals from their sphere alone without a database, the upcoming paragraphs will instead discuss and stress the importance of an organized database.

The average real estate sales person will close deals with 7% of the people in their database every year. (A great sales person will double or even triple that.) That means that if you can get an extra 100 quality contacts from Facebook into your database, and market to them, you will be able to close an extra 7 transactions.

Caveat 1: *Garbage in, garbage out. Only put people in your database if you know them, or have had a conversation with them at some point in recent history. If you haven't, start a conversation and then add them when they communicate back to you.*

Caveat 2: *Having someone in your database will do no good if you don't time block to send some form of communication to them.*

A good sales person can often get a referral off every other closed deal (often referred to as the snowball effect). Adding just 5 people per week to your database would give you somewhere around 260 new contacts for the year, giving you a realistic chance of closing deals with 18 of them. If one in every two refers you to someone new, that could be 27 total transactions, not counting the referrals from the referrals and so on.

Explode Your Growth

To really expand your database, combine the method above with the aforementioned Facebook messaging strategy. As you go through your time blocked process of combing through Facebook and other social sources to add people to your database, you can send them a personal Facebook message at the same time (remember if you need something to talk about, start by looking at what they have recently posted and use that as a conversation starter).

Think of this as a game of rolling dice, you will not get a lead off every message; however, the more messages you send, (or in this analogy dice you roll), the more total chances you will have of winning big. But at the very least you will have lots of small victories as you add people to your database after your conversations.

INSTAGRAM

———

We are currently living in a digitally driven world and both home buyers and sellers are spending more time checking social media than ever before. Some may say that Instagram is just another platform to keep up with, but it has the potential to be incredibly effective for your real estate business if you use it consistently. There are no set rules for how real estate professionals should be using Instagram, but if the platform has the possibility to target a perfect prospect or allows you to stay in front of past clients, friends, and family... why not join the party?

It is important to think of Instagram as a way to brand your social identity to gain business. In recent years Instagram has dominated screentime for users, especially those in the 18-35 market. Here are some tips and best practices for growing your business brand on your Instagram.

Switch Your Instagram Profile To A Business Account

The option to switch allows you to have better tools and functionality at your disposal. As soon as you change to a business profile, you will have access to insights on your posts and stories. Insights allow you to view the engagement on your posts, impressions, audience demographic and more. In addition, business accounts have call to action buttons that are displayed on your profile page. These buttons could for instance say: Call, Email, Directions, etc. Making the buttons useful calls to action help to make contacting you easier.

How to switch your personal account to a business profile:

1. Open the app and click on the drop-down menu on the top right of the screen

2. Click settings

3. In the settings menu, click account, and at the bottom you will then see "switch to a business account"

4. Once you click that option, you will be guided through details to add additional information to your profile.

Switching back to a personal account is possible. It is recommended though that you stick to a business profile if you are trying to act as a brand.

Benefits Of A Business Account

You are much more likely to be contacted! *An online prospect can easily click a button and choose whether they want to email you, call you, send a message, or find your business location — all without having to leave the app.*

Access to insights. *Yes, these insights are minimal, but your real estate business can still benefit from this information. It is a quick way for you to get a better look at who is viewing your profile and how your content is working for you. To access the insights, go to your profile page, or a post on your profile, and click the insights data listed on the top of your account. You will then see impression, reach, and follower information within the past week.*

Ads. *With a business account, you can run your current Facebook ads to your Instagram feed without additional set up. This increases engagement, allows your ad to receive higher conversion rates, and you can reach a larger target audience on the platform that they are spending more of their time on.*

Best Practices On Instagram For Marketing Success

So you have an Instagram business profile, what should you post?

1. Post photos and videos that you recorded. No one wants to see a profile full of stock photos!
2. Post the best photo of your listing. What is the most unique part of the home? It doesn't just have to be the front of the home.
3. Show off your personal side from time to time, especially on stories! A day in the life of...
4. Take advantage of relevant hashtags — both popular and local ones. Come up with your own personal hashtag as well. An easy way to get better with hashtags is to save frequently used lists of hashtags in the notes section on your phone. Here are some hashtags you can use:

#realestate, #realtor, #homebuyers, #homebuying, #homeforsale, #YOURCITYlocalbusiness, #YOURCITY+STATE, #realestateagent, #closingday, #buyeragent, #realestatelife, #newlisting, #selleragent, #newlistingalert, #firsttimehomebuyers, #localbusiness, #homes, #homedecor, #homegoals, #homesweethome, #homesforsale, #homebuyingCITY, #YOURCITYrealestate, #property, #investment, #realestategoals, #realestateexpert, #realestatebroker...

5. Respond to post comments and reply to your followers' posts. Communication, even on social media, is a two-way street.

6. Do not worry about when and when not to post, or how many posts you should do a week. Listen to your audience and find your niche. There are some sites that can allow you to schedule posts on Instagram if it feels more like a job than a hobby.

7. Make sure your post captions occasionally mention your target audience and the area. Following that same line, tell a little tale or story about the home.

8. Make sure your bio is something that will grab attention of users. Using Emojis never hurts, they can only make your posts stand out more.

9. If your clients allow, post a photo from closing and tag them in it.

10. Everyone loves to hear about a funny real estate story, or something humorous you came across in a home you were touring. Share it!

11. Give tips and tricks for first time homebuyers or sellers — share staging pictures, home DIY projects, spring cleaning tips, mortgage options, etc.

12. Walkthrough videos of your open house are always fun for stories.

13. A great feature on Instagram is the location setting. Tagging the location in your photos can lead to more shares and features.

With consistency, your Instagram business profile will allow you to better build relationships and you will have additional control over your brand and business.

LINKEDIN

LinkedIn makes it easier than any other website to download a list of all your contacts in just a few clicks. Like we discussed with Facebook, it is a ton of work to slowly and manually export all of your contacts (which if you haven't done already you absolutely should!) Where Facebook makes it tough by forcing you to do the work manually, LinkedIn is built for business and makes downloading your contacts into an organized list a cinch.

TANGIBLE ACTIVITY:

Start the Download. Go to *www.LinkedIn.com/mynetwork/contacts/* go to the right of the screen and click "export contacts".[14]

Or from the home page click on:

1. "My Network"

2. "See all" on the top left

3. "Manage Synced and Imported Contacts" on the top right

4. "Export Contacts" on the bottom right

5. It will let you choose which data you want to download

The result from the above steps will be a downloaded list of all your contacts with email addresses and some other valuable information. This is something that has been around for years, and it will likely one day go away as marketers continue to exploit it. For now, this is something I strongly suggest you take advantage of!

Once you download your contacts, scan that list and delete anyone who you do not think is going to be a potential lead source. Keep in mind that sometimes you just never know who might be a lead or who might not. Next, with those who remain, add a column and sort each person into a group (if your current database/sphere of influence list currently uses groups, uses these same group names). The idea is to take your download and to make the data as clean and organized as possible before adding it to your main CRM or database list.

[14] Every few months/years the process for downloading LinkedIn contacts changes. If the above method doesn't work for you, a quick Google search should reveal a new method.

LinkedIn Messages

Remember the Facebook messaging strategy? The same strategy in theory works on LinkedIn also, but not as well in this case. This is because of the usage differences between Facebook and LinkedIn. As much as I hate to say it, I think many of us know that LinkedIn has kind of become the one social media site that everybody has, but that less people "actively" use, and LinkedIn messages seem to get lost in the shuffle because when people get them, they are primed to expect spam and other less than genuine sales attempts.

Think about it, when was the last time you checked your LinkedIn? I do know sales people who are extremely successful on LinkedIn; however, a lot of people do not use it as much.

PRO TIP: *Food For Thought — We mention above that "active" usage may be declining on LinkedIn; however, for every social site in decline, there is another one in growth mode. At the time of writing this many of my colleagues and I have been setting numerous meetings per month off of Instagram (owned by Facebook). The same logic we discuss with Facebook can be applied to almost any social medium with a few tweaks.*

Another Bonus With LinkedIn

Another cool thing about LinkedIn is that it gives you everyone's job titles, as well as their experience, so you know a little more about them. Sure, Facebook and many other sites offer some job titles as well, but many that we have seen also include aliases for names, and less than accurate job titles.

Why do job titles matter? They matter when it comes to sales and prospecting and we have a full section dedicated to why.

JOB TITLES

____

How Can You Prospect With Job Titles? Simple — Get Creative

How Can You Prospect With Job Titles? Simple — Get Creative

Almost every person in the world could be a referral source if you figure out how to best utilize them. Not only could they be a referral source to you, but you could also be a referral source to them. Although this can be true in all aspects of life, starting with how you could add professional value through your or their job is a good start.

Try to think of each person's job and how you could work with them or add value to their life. For instance, maybe you see someone who lists their job title as a financial planner. Financial planners deal with people's money, and you are dealing with people's houses. People's houses are worth a lot of money. Financial planners typically strive to give people a return on investment. You could talk to financial planners and get referrals to their clients who want to diversify and get into investment properties. You, in turn, can connect them with and help them get into contact with people you work with who need financial advice, even if it's just a strategy to begin saving for a home.

The beauty of job titles is that there is opportunity everywhere, you just have to apply some critical thinking. For instance, if someone works at a jewelry store, they know people who are getting engaged. Those people are prime targets to buy houses in the near future. People in human resources know people who are getting hired to the area, a sign that they might be in the market for somewhere different to live. Look at every job title out there and be creative. Put together a strategy for how to market towards each of your connections based on what they do. The key will be to take these relationships off LinkedIn and the web and into real life meetings.

Every single person out there can somehow be a referral partner. You just need to get creative. Once you spot an opportunity for someone who you could refer to or get referrals from, the next step is to teach them how to refer to you. We will cover this more in a later section that focuses on the power of a strong referral.

TANGIBLE ACTIVITY:

Timeblock five minutes now for this LinkedIn activity (and then set it on repeat)

This five-minute activity is all about looking for job changes. LinkedIn makes it easier than any other site to see when someone changes jobs. In fact, if you go to your notifications tab, one of the first things you are going to see from the app is, "Congratulate others for starting new positions." If you click "see new positions," you can then see the job title and company that your connections transitioned to.

I think we all know that in real estate, a new job is a huge buying sign. If someone gets a new job, there is a good chance they might be moving in the near future. Whether they want to move to be closer to the new job or they feel like their new salary warrants a better living condition, it is a buying sign you can't afford to ignore. Most marketers here would begin rattling off ways for you to start annoying these people, or give you a 5 paragraph script to send them in a LinkedIn message (a great way to get blocked). Don't do anything spammy. Simply send an email, a personal phone call, maybe even a handwritten note, just make sure to do something. Congratulate the person on their new job, get the conversation rolling and let them know you care. Then set a follow up in your calendar for 2-3 weeks from then to follow up again via phone. Stay on top of it, but in a non-spammy way.

This is free data that LinkedIn is giving you that you can use and harness to your advantage. If you have an assistant, this even can be a great task for them. They can even pre-write a note for you to send to your connections on job changes.

BUILDING RAPPORT

3 Tangible Ideas For Rapport Research Using Social Media

A couple of years ago an agent stopped me at a conference and asked me a question. He asked if there were any good business practices for using social media for sales people who weren't interested in lead generation. I didn't think much of it at the time, but looking back I realize it was brilliant. I thought it was a strange question because who on earth doesn't want more leads?! But upon chatting with him for longer, I began to understand his situation. He was a top producer who, at this point in his career, was working by referral only and doing well. He wanted to use social media, but not to generate new leads/contacts, but rather to go deeper with his existing audience. After talking for almost an hour, we outlined a perfect plan of attack for him. He could use Facebook and LinkedIn to learn more about his customers as a way to build rapport, and increase his chances of converting more friends and past clients into repeat business.

If I was about to go to a listing presentation or if I was about to go into a meeting with a new client to hopefully win their business, I would do everything I could to maximize my chances of that person liking me, and thus increasing my chances of getting the deal. One of the easiest ways to do this is to look on LinkedIn, Facebook, or your preferred social engine and seek out conversation topics as well as to conduct general research on your prospects even if you already know them.

3 Tangible Ideas For Rapport Research Using Social Media

1. Look at your target's interests, and figure out things to talk about that will make you more similar or interesting to them. Similarity increases your chances of engagement.

2. Look at what they have posted recently. If they were interested enough in something to post about it, it will be a surefire way to initiate an engaging conversation.

3. Look to see if you have friends in common and who. This may give you the opportunity to ask mutual friends to put a good word in for you.

Using social media for research doesn't just work for prospecting your database, it also greatly helps when working with lower quality online leads. If I get a lead online, such as one from Zillow or Facebook, and find that we have six friends in common, I could reach out to those six friends to see if anyone knows them (the lead) well. Imagine how your chances of setting an appointment would increase if a mutual friend had already mentioned to the lead that you happened to be amazing or trustworthy. With commissions as high as they are in our industry, any activities you can do, or tools you can use to increase your chances of success, are well worth it.

A football team doesn't show up to the game and just expect to win. They watch film, study opponents past behavior, and do everything else in their power to hope-fully bring home a win. And that's exactly what you need to do to bring home your own wins.

OLD SCHOOL MARKETING WITH NEW SCHOOL KNOWLEDGE & STRATEGY

———

We talked a lot about using different social media channels and digital marketing to get leads, but digital marketing, despite being a shiny new object, is not the only set of options when it comes to making new connections and getting business. Anyone who has been in the business for more than 10 years probably remembers the time when a large portion of the business that you gathered was from offline sources, print marketing, door to door, networking, and other traditional strategies.

These "offline" marketing strategies, despite having fallen out of fashion a little, are worth understanding. Many of them still not only work, but also have a high ROI. These strategies are often more labor intensive and sometimes more costly, two conditions that prevent others in your industry from starting or continuing. These barriers to entry, whether real or perceived, create the perfect window for you to break in by using some creativity and grit to find success.

When you think about the fact that online marketing has been so prevalent and so talked about for the last 10 years, you have to remember that fewer people (especially newer agents) are doing some of these old-school techniques. As digital marketing doubles in cost every few years, while traditional marketing stays flat, more people may begin going back to basics.

No conversation about old school marketing would be complete without discussing a term whose very name suggests that it is old, labor intensive and time consuming. This concept is called farming. It has evolved over the decades to become an all encompassing term for blanketing a certain geographic area with marketing efforts in the hopes of generating a business outcome.

SECTION 11

FARMING & MAILERS

The very word farming conjures up notions of antiquated practices that are labor intensive but offer varying crop yields based on market and weather conditions. Farming in real estate may be similar, and it still has one of the highest ROI's depending on how you execute it. Farming in real estate is the practice of prospecting for business around a geographic area. Your "farm" is the area you isolate and then repeatedly tend to, by marketing to the people who live there with mailers, door knocks, community events, etc.

The big differentiator between traditional marketing (the "farming" your ancestors may have done) VS. what you can do today, is that now you have digital tools to augment and improve your strategies.

Where Should I Farm? Is It Even Worth It?

When you are thinking about whether to farm a certain area (we're talking the marketing type of farming, where you are going to systematically mail, make calls, or door knock a certain geographic area) it becomes important to first isolate the area or areas that are ripe with opportunity, or to isolate those areas in which you may have a competitive edge.

Where To Start? Set A Budget And Get The Data

When you want to start marketing to a certain geographic area, the best thing to do is to find one that fits your budget. What I mean by this is you have to find an area where the number of houses is going to be affordable to market to, both in terms of your time and in terms of postage. Postage is just a fancy word for money coupons disguised as stickers. Basically, the amount of postage you need is going to become a large portion of your budget.

Finding a budget that makes sense should really be the starting point for any marketing objective. If you are going to mail to these farm areas three, four, five times a year, ask how much can you afford in postage, mailing expenses, etc. and look at how this compares to your potential ROI. Each stamp in the U.S. (at the time I am writing this) is 35 cents for a postcard and 55 cents for a letter. Cheaper rates are of course available for bulk mailers. Personally, I think letters work a whole lot better than postcards because if you get someone to physically open something, they are already a little bit emotionally invested in reading what you have to say, but we will delve more into types of mailers in a later section.

If setting your budget seems hard, and you are unsure about the general size of the area you want to mail to, you could instead start by pulling the data of the homes you want to mail to. This might give you a better idea of what you can afford. One way technology has jumped in to make farming easier, is by giving us access to software that will enable users to circle a neighborhood online or on an app, and download all of the names/addresses and other public info in a neat spreadsheet.

If you don't already have a good tool for easily pulling data, consider asking your favorite title company. There are a lot of title companies out there who have different apps and softwares that real estate professionals can use to pull addresses, owner names, phone numbers, and sometimes even mortgage information (helpful to figure out how long people have been in the neighborhood and how much they could pocket after selling their home in today's economy). If you don't have a title company resource, consider looking to see what tools your county offers on their website for free, or check out the NextDoor App[15] which may have names and addresses for bigger developments and communities. These last two options will not be as easy, and may require some manual data entry, but you can always find a high school or college kid eager to help for some cash.

Consider that some areas have higher turn over all of the time, while other areas tend to remain stagnant for years. When thinking about the "where" it is also important to look to see if any one or two agents dominate the area already. If after research it does appear that another agent(s) already dominates the area in terms of actual sales, you will need either a unique approach, deeper pockets or a novel value proposition to start edging in using farming.

Now that you have the contact information of the people you hope to market to as well as a budget and a plan, the next step is to figure out a plan to evaluate your results when you are done. This must be done before your marketing starts, so that you have indicators along the way of when to keep going and when to pivot your strategy or fold. Figure out a plan for how you are going to evaluate your efforts and then make a plan for the following quarter or year to stop, modify or continue based on the objectives and results you wrote down ahead of time. You cannot mail, call, or door knock a neighborhood once, in a haphazard fashion and then proclaim that it didn't work. You first have to figure out what success will look like, and then figure out the amount of work it will take to get there. Does success look like getting phone calls or does it look like specifically getting new listings or picking up new buyers? Set some clear evaluation points ahead of time with different types of measurable objectives that will make your decision of where to spend your marketing time and money easier.

Postcards VS. Letters: Things To Consider

If you do postcards, make them as funny as possible or as eye-catching as possible, and you will have a slightly better success rate. But be aware that if you are mailing to a higher end demographic where there are a lot of children or a lot of high school kids, postcards become especially tough because a lot of people in that demographic will have their kids grab the mail on their way home from school. Kids, especially teenagers, know better than anyone what is junk mail, and they will throw it away as a service to their parents before the parents even see it. With a letter, there is a higher chance that the letter will actually make it into the hands of the adult.

Tangible Tips, Tricks, And Steps For Mailers

Tip 1: Pull a list of addresses from a local title company website or app.

Tip 2: Scrub that list to make sure you are only mailing to residential addresses. Also, to make sure you are only mailing to people, make sure you are sending the letter to the mailing address for the house, not necessarily the property address, keeping in mind that a lot of places are not owner-occupied in many markets.

Tip 3: Some of the lists you procure might include phone numbers. If so, and if you plan to use them, make sure to scrub that against the Do Not Call registry and your local multiple listing services (to see if they are expired listings with do not solicit requests).

Tip 4: Check your local association and or your broker/boss for rules on disclaimers you may need to include in your mailings. In some markets, agents are required to say something to the extent of "If your home is currently listed, this is not intended to solicit that listing." Similarly, lenders, financial advisors, and insurance agents likely have many mandatory disclaimers and requirements.

Tip 5: Use cheesy, personal return address labels. More explanation below.

Tip 6: Hand write things on an envelope or outside of postcard whenever time permits. More explanation below.

Tip 7: Plan to mail to your group more than once or else plan to fail.

Keeping Up Appearances

When it comes to mailers, especially those you want people to open the most, the important thing is the envelope. After all, if nobody opens it what's the point? But the risk/reward is higher with letters than postcards because if you do actually convince someone to open your envelope you already have won their attention for at least a few seconds. So what can you do to your envelope to increase your chances? The answer is to make it look as personal and non-business as possible. Just go home tonight and look at the spam letters you will undoubtedly have from insurance companies, quick high-interest loan companies etc., and think about how you can make your envelope as different and personal as possible.

I usually tell people to either hand write the return address on the envelope or use fun, personalized address stickers that you and your family might get around the holidays or from charities. The goal here is that you do not want it to look like business mail. If your letter to them says, "Mortgage Company" on the return address, the chance of people opening it is going to go down significantly unless they are already in a transaction with you.

Every day I receive 2-3 letters from insurance agencies that I do not work with trying to get my business. In the last six years, I do not think I have opened a single one. The reason is that I do not work with them. They have nothing pertinent to tell me, and I really just do not care what is in the letter. However, on the occasion that I am goaded into opening something, is because I did not know who it was from, then

I do occasionally read the message. All in all, unless your business name invokes pure excitement and curiosity in the average human, consider using your name and a residential address instead of your logo and office address for the return area.

For the actual address of the recipient, try to make sure that you are either using very professional trendy address labels or that you write them with your own handwriting. If you have an assistant, a secretary at your office, a spouse, a teenager, a high school kid-next-door that can physically write these, pay them to write it, but make sure it is legible. Handwriting will exponentially increase the chances of your stuff getting read. Who does not love opening mail that has a handwritten address and a non-business feel to it? Sure, there are machines and services that make the envelope look handwritten, but 90% of the time customers can tell. There is just something unmistakably imperfect about a personal letter in the mail. Maybe even take a second to lick the stamp and put it on the envelope just a little bit crooked or less than perfect to add a human touch.

Warning: Don't lick too many envelopes if you or your business partner purchased the cheapest envelopes in the store.[16]

A Tale Of Two Mailers

Below are two scenarios of mailers that I worked on with agents. Each story breaks down the general concept on the mailer, amount spent, and the ROI. You can use each example to better plan the direction you want mailers to take you, but also to plan a realistic ROI.

Mailer 1:
In 2015 I helped an agent with a postcard that was simple but effective. The front said, "You might not know me, but I've been inside your house." The back said. "No, I'm not a peeping Tom or social deviant, I'm a local Realtor and over the last 30 years I have listed, sold, and toured over 1200 of your neighborhood's 1300 homes... Nobody knows 'Neighborhood Name' like me..." Then it was her picture, a cute loving older woman. Her picture actually made the postcard a whole lot less creepy then if it were a slick, 35-year-old dude. It was funny, attention getting, kind of weird, and it worked like a charm. After mailing to 1300 homes for a price of about $800 she actually picked up 3 sales, all over $250,000. In one of my follow up meetings with this agent one year later, she happily reported that one of the transactions happened to

 [16] See reference: Seinfeld, Season 7 Episode 22; 26 May, 1996.

be with an investor who had since listed and sold another 2 investment properties in the same area with her. I don't know the exact amount she earned in commission off of the postcards, however, based on average price points in the area she likely took home around $40,000 before expenses off $2400 in postcards that year (with 3 mailings).

Mailer 2:

In 2017, I worked with an agent who had purchased access to a software provider who told her which homes in her farm area were most likely to sell soon based on some predictive analytics. They took her farm area of 1,000 homes and told her which 200 to focus her time on. They then mailed to these homes 6 times with a mixture of postcards and letters. She spent about $600/mo for 6 months for a total of $3,600. The average price point in her farm area was $400,000. They also recommended that she door knock. After 6 months she ended the relationship; she had received 5 good inquiries, 1 of which had closed. She earned a commission around $12,000 (before broker fees) and is still working the other 4 leads hoping they turn into something. The interesting thing about using predictive analytics is that based on the price of the data it may have been cheaper for her to market to the entire 1,000 homes rather than the top 20%. She still made a fair ROI, but it wasn't as exciting as the first example.

In both of the above examples the main commonality that many people overlook when marketing is frequency. Neither agent mailed once and then gave up. They repeated their strategy with slightly different verbiage and messaging, but similar branding. The number of times that your target is exposed to your advertisement is called the frequency. Although you can get lucky on the first try, a higher frequency will usually net you better overall results.

The biggest question I usually get from agents is regarding how often is too often to mail to your farm. This comes down to 2 factors: How annoying you want to be? AND How much do you want to spend? In a hot market, mailing something different once a month can be pretty non-invasive if you can afford to keep up with it, especially before the first commission check rolls in. The people who are interested will call you, and the people who aren't will throw your mailer right out usually without worrying about it. Although, if you get lucky, you may get a call from a crazy person once a year telling you to stop mailing to them, and yelling at you about how you got their information in the first place. If it is your own neighborhood, an area where people know you, a quarterly mailer can work just fine.

If you are still unsure how many mailers you should send out, think about the possible return on your investment (and time). If you are marketing in a neighborhood that has property values around $80,000, look at what your commission would be if one of these postcards or letters worked. Then look at what that would equal out to after your split with your broker, and after any of your other hard costs are spent. Is that worth it versus the $300,000, $400,000 or $500,000 neighborhoods, where if you market something for an entire year and you do not get a lead, but then you finally you could get one sale, that will pay for all the previous marketing that you have done. That being said if the $80,000–$120,000 neighborhood has high turnover, and you can succeed based on total deals, then you could have a goldmine. More units equal more referrals and a bigger database. At the end of the day, the answer to how many times you should mail out will depend, but it is more than once and less than every day.

If farming/mailing is starting to sound too monumental or you are not sure which neighborhood to start with, the first option I always suggest is your personal neighborhood. I like to call this strategy The Neighborhood Letter.

The Neighborhood Letter

The name alone is pretty self-explanatory, and for those sales professionals who live in a traditional neighborhood or building, this is the best ROI for any mailer that I have seen. The reason it can work so well is simple, you are starting off with better odds. In traditional marketing the first few "impressions" you get in front of a random person help you to establish credibility, trust, and familiarity. When you start your marketing efforts to people who live close by to you, or to those who are part of a certain group (e.g. a neighborhood or association who might be vaguely familiar with you or be more likely based on shared proximity to have something in common with you) you are starting ahead of the traditional marketing curve, thus marketing with higher odds of success.

When sending something to your neighborhood, you already have something in common with them: you are one of their neighbors. Not only do you live close, you likely share many people in your social circles. The goal here is to find a way to offer them as much value as possible. As a Realtor or lender, one of the biggest value propositions you likely have is access to, and knowledge about, local market data. Below is a version of the neighborhood letter that I have helped agents and lenders use 50+ times that has delivered leads in all markets we have tested it in. The idea is for you to tweak and personalize it to make the letter sound like you, and to make it appeal more specifically to your neighborhood. Below we will outline the exact letter some have used and seen success with. Take it, modify it, and make it your own.

Part 1:

> *"Hey, [first name] (or another regionally appropriate semi-informal greeting)*
>
> *I hope all is well. My name is: [your name]. I am one of your neighbors and also a Realtor. I just wanted to send you a quick letter to let you know a couple quick updates. Home prices in our neighborhood have never been higher (only put this if it is true). They are currently up 'X' percent over the last year and 'X' percent over two years ago."*

Now, obviously, here you do not want to lie. Please look up correct statistics from your local market. People love statistics and love true numbers. You know, most people's biggest investment is their house; however, most Realtors are not sending quarterly or monthly estimates of what consumer's homes are worth. In the bottom of the letter, include a short list of the most recent five home transactions in the area, giving numbers for beds, baths, square footage, sold prices, and any other information that might be pertinent. You do not necessarily have to include pictures or anything crazy. Keep it simple. The shorter this letter is, the better it is going to work. After all of the good info, just include a nice closing, ideally with something memorable about you and a question to them.

Part 2:

> *"I just wanted to give you this quick real estate update. If you ever want to know exactly what your home might be worth, just let me know any updates you have recently done to your home so I can adjust my market stats and make the final number more specific to your home.*
>
> *Your neighbor,*
> *[signature]*
> *[contact info]"*

The reason that you should ask what updates they have done is that everybody loves to brag about what they have done to their house. Who wouldn't? Simply by asking them what updates they have recently done and offering them a reward (the updated information for their home), you are increasing the chances that they are going to reach out to you. It changes the close from a hard "call me to sell your house" to a softer "just call me to talk, I'm interested". Being interested in someone else is the first step to making them interested in you.

The overall idea is to keep the letter as short as possible so people don't feel overwhelmed when they open it; however, below are some items that agents have added over the years that they have had success with. I wouldn't recommend doing all of them at once, but instead A/B testing[17] what works best in your area over the course of the year until you find the combination, and eventually the total letter, that delivers the best results.

Add-On Suggestion 1:
A slight tweak that some agents ad is to make a harder offer for a free home estimate. Some agents will even say that they are practicing their home estimation skills and want people who are interested in knowing their home values.

Add-On Suggestion 2:
Another possible addition is to make an appeal to the recipient's sense of community. Feel free to let them know that if they want to choose their new neighbors, you could help any of their friends try to find a home in the neighborhood as well.

Add-On Suggestion 3:
Real estate marketing can be pretty cold, so one way to make your letter more personable is to add a personal bio with a picture of yourself or your family. The bio would include a few paragraphs about who you are personally and professionally. The goal here is to give people reasons to call you other than the fact that you are trying to sell them something. It's kind of like fishing, the more fun personal details (pieces of bait) you include, the greater the chance you will get a bite by someone resonating with your points enough to take action and call you.

Add-On Suggestion 4:
"P.S. if you see me driving around in my [insert car name here] make sure to wave." **OR** *"P.S. If you see me walking my [insert dog breed and name] around the neighborhood come over! We are friendly." Adding something like this is a great way to end the letter so people will remember you for something other than real estate.*

---

[17] A/B Testing is traditionally a digital marketing practice where you compare two different items on a web page to see which yields better results. The same concept applies with letters.

Overall, the concept is the same no matter where you live or what you actually plan to say. Start personal, give some good information, and then end personal.

Farming With A Purpose: Be Specific

Many sales people and marketers take the same approach to their mailings that my toddler takes towards his meals, that is, throwing everything at the wall. He isn't trying to be malicious (and neither are the sales people). The root cause is that both my son and the sales people know that they should be doing something, they just aren't exactly sure what. In this case, we presented our son with food, and he figures "one possible application of this food is as a projectile." In the case of the sales person, a broker/friend/colleague/coach told them to do some marketing, so they did a bunch of postcards and waited to see what would happen. This type of marketing is unlikely to be fruitful, but when you add purpose to it, it goes from throwing food at the wall haphazardly to throwing a dart right at the bullseye.

One of the best examples of purposeful farming that I have seen recently in the real estate industry is when an agent uses existing buyers and sellers (either their own or someone else's) as ammunition to pick up new buyers and other listings. Although this strategy could be done better with door knocking or phone calls, letters typically end up being the most time effective option.

A real life example of using buyers or sellers you have as ammunition actually exists in the wild outside of a specific strategy. Just think about it, when you are busy, you typically attract more business (albeit at a time when you feel like you can barely keep up). This phenomenon happens partly because being busy attracts more business, but it's also because in real estate, every client you have working with you, and every listing with your name attached to it, is virtually a free advertisement or billboard. Once you get a ball rolling it's easier to keep it going because you have built momentum. Marketing and business work in the same way. The next tip uses this overall concept but puts a strategic push behind it to amplify the results.

The Best Ammo

1. Your buyers who can't find homes

2. Your sellers

3. Buyers who are working with a busy agent in your office

4. Literally any listing

5. Your recent past customers

For most people, having buyers who can't find homes is a problem; however, for those agents who can see this as an opportunity, it can be a goldmine for getting listings and meeting new people. If I had 12 clients who could not find houses out there, I would write down where each of them really wants to be, kind of like a dream neighborhood list.

Then, I would pull addresses for those areas, maybe for four or five streets around their target area and then would put together a very professional letter.

And the letter might say something like this:

> *"Hey [first name],*
>
> *My name is [your name]. I am a local Realtor. I just wanted to let you know, my two clients, [first names] just moved here from [city name], and they are really interested in living in your neighborhood. Nothing is currently on the market, so I just wanted to let you know that if you or someone you know is thinking about selling, I might be able to get you a lucrative offer. If you have any questions or are even a little bit curious as to what that offer might be be, please call me.*
>
> *My clients would absolutely love to be in your neighborhood.*
>
> *Talk soon,*
> *[your name]*
> *[your phone number]"*

Similar to the neighborhood letter, some people will spice this up with specific stats or even info about the clients (make sure to watch out for fair housing violations with some personal details). Some agents will even send the letter themselves but written as if they themselves were the clients. The logic here being that there is a lower chance of the letter being thrown away as marketing if it is person to person simply because of the extra emotional appeal when its one person to another. I would only recommend doing this with your client's explicit permission, but in most cases, clients are eager for their agent to test out any idea that might help them nab the perfect off-market home. The major win here is that finding a client a home that isn't listed takes you from being a good agent to an absolute super hero that they will tell everyone they know about.

Many people would say that this strategy is similar to any other mailer you would do and that you could just say you have buyers looking when you don't. The idea is that a specific marketing offer about real buyers, or from a real buyer is always going to be a better marketing piece than a random letter asking someone to sell.

When you mention your client's names and where they are moving from, it becomes much more real, and it also becomes much more likely that you will get a response. Last year I advised an agent on a mailing campaign and based on her goals, we used the logic above to prospect for homes for her very specific buyers. She had clients who wanted a home on a small but expensive lake near us. There were only 75 homes in the area that fit what the buyers wanted. I helped strategize with the agent to send out handwritten notes to all 75 people whose lots/homes matched the buyers wants (having pulled the list from a local title company app). Within 10 days the agent had received over 10 phone calls from potential sellers we had mailed to. Now, she did not actually end up finding a house for those clients through the campaign, but she did pick up multiple listings and buyers off of that letter. It was still a win-win for her. She not only did something tangible to show her buyers the value of the work she was putting in for them, but it also helped her to pick up additional business that she would not have had without the tangible ammunition these buyers provided.

 If you are a new agent and don't have any buyers yet to use as ammunition, consider asking other agents in your office for their buyer needs, and use that as ammunition. It gives you a reason to prospect that's more tangible than simply asking for business and more random prospecting it's a win. Not only will you forge valuable relationships with more experienced agents in your office, but it will put you on the fast track to having business.

The buy side is pretty easy to figure out; every buyer has wants and needs and you can mention that to potential sellers who may be excited to brag about how their home is perfect in every way possible. On the list side, the same general strategy works, but with a twist. In fact, a version of this strategy has been employed by agents since before I was born. This prehistoric form of marketing by using listings as ammunition was the "Just Listed" postcard. For the first few years that I worked in real estate marketing, agents would ask me to help craft these postcards almost every week. At each subsequent meeting with agents who sent out just listed postcards, I would ask if they generated any business. I would usually hear that they didn't generate leads; however, after compiling more data it seemed like 1 in every few thousand that were mailed out would generate a phone call or two. Some even generated an actual deal. My main reason for sharing these numbers is to explain that without an extremely clever message, these postcards were so over done that their success rates were minimal.

Although results from just listed/just sold mailers were low, the overall concept and message still has some value.

Taking this "new listing near you" strategy applying it in a way that has a much higher chance of success would be to use it to go door to door. For instance, if you sign a new listing agreement with a local family at 6pm you could go and door knock the nearest 25 homes afterward.

This is the script I would roll with:

> *"Hey,*
>
> *I am [your name], the Realtor. I just listed your neighbor, [client's name]'s house and I wanted you to be the first to know so that you have the opportunity to let any friends know who might be hoping to move to the area. Similarly, if you want to know exactly what your home is worth, I would love to help you figure that out."*

The idea here is to make use of the law of numbers. Anytime a house sells, there is an increased chance that another home is going to sell within the nearest 25-50 houses in the next six months if not sooner. If you do plan to door knock, also bring flyers with you containing all recent home sale data, and be sure to look for FSBOs (for sale by owners) to include as well because this is a great way to include value the home owner wouldn't have already known about from normal online sites. If the homeowner did know about the FSBO values already, then although you may not be presenting any new information, at least you will be prepared.

I know that talking about a strategy that involves door knocking and mailings in 2019 may seem antiquated, but I cannot emphasize enough the potential that these strategies have when done systematically. Especially when compared to other agents who spend marketing dollars on costly online leads with low ROI's, the agents who door knock on a consistent basis and bring valuable information will get more business for less money.

There are so many people who are spending thousands of dollars on Zillow every year, and they complain, saying, "The leads are not good. It is so expensive."

I work with an agent who door knocks at least 7-10 hours per week in specific neighborhoods. He keeps detailed notes on the areas that he door knocks, the houses that answer the door, the houses that did not, and the relationships he makes. His database has grown in the last five years from zero to over 3,000 people, all in the same city, and he is now averaging well over $15 million a year in sales, and much of it started with the door knocking technique.

It Pays To Take Stock Before You Knock

Putting my cheesy but cleverly rhymed title aside, if you do decide to go door knocking, I always recommend doing your homework first. What I mean by this is that you want to make sure you have good information and a good presentation ready in case someone actually answers the door. I have seen so many times where a sales person goes door knocking fully expecting no one to answer the door. If you go into it with that mindset, it is not going to work. Make sure to have some handouts that have tangible and updated local information (part of your ammunition). Think about what you are about to hand someone, it is something they will care about? If the answer is no then do not hand it out.

Property, city, and neighborhood-specific home statistics are the best possible options for tangible data. What you want to do is pull a list of the nearest 25-50 homes that have sold and include data on bedrooms, bathrooms, square footage, everything you can think of. Have that on a flyer. To ensure you are prepared for other off the cuff conversations, be sure to have apps on your phone that can pull other data as well. If you don't have better, or faster access to data than the people you are visiting, what value are you really bringing?

If it is a neighborhood where you really, really want to have some success, go above and beyond. Try bringing a pack of 100 oversized manila or orange legal type envelopes and put a short, handwritten note to each homeowner inside of it. Leave it in their door unless there is a no soliciting sign. Remember you can not put things in mailboxes in most municipalities without actually mailing them with postage. Unless you are looking to use legal trouble as a networking opportunity, check local ordinances first. If the homes you are visiting have that little newspaper insert under their mailbox, that is usually fair game. Anything you can leave behind is huge. I have worked with sales people in the past who had a habit of leaving 100 Grand candy bars for every 100k the home is worth and leaving the candy with a short note that said, "I want to get you $250,000 for your house." For a 250k house, you could leave 2 full-size bars and a fun size. This approach would be a good mix of tangible and memorable.

Note: *Please do not do this in super warm weather. The author of this book does not want to be responsible for melted chocolate all over someone's front porch. It's more of a fair weather marketing strategy.*

A lot of people say that they do not like door knocking because they do not feel safe or because it is not in their comfort zone. If this is the case for you, figure out a way to make it more comfortable with a few adjustments. One fun way to do this involves your family. If you have kids, they are likely selling something for some fundraiser, maybe it's delicious Girl Scout Cookies, Cub Scout Popcorn, or some type of coupon book. Schools and official groups prey on cute kids to sell things for a constant barrage of fundraisers. They use kids as a vehicle because cute kids are sales gold. I, by the way, was one of the top sales children in Cub Scout Pack 1384 in the mid-90s. My sales record was fantastic and it was an overall great experience. Until I was 10 years old my mom or dad would usually hang out in the car or by the sidewalk while I approached the homes of prospective customers. Reflecting back, this made me think: if they were selling something, they could have come with me and try to hawk their wares as well. Plus once someone sells their home they may have a lot more cash to buy popcorn and cookies from your kids.

Although this strategy ranks pretty high on the obnoxious scale, it is a good opportunity to spend some time with your kids, teach them some valuable lessons about sales, and increase your chances of people opening the door by bringing a cute kid with you. However amazing and charismatic that you think you are, your child is cuter and more approachable. Have a kid that's too little to sell things? Bring them in a wagon—as long as they aren't screaming, it will make you look more neighborly and approachable. Or maybe you are a dog owner. Door knocking with your 4 legged fur child will help you give off a similar cute/approachable vibe as well.

Whether you decide to door knock by yourself or with a group, it is important to pick the times of day you decide to go out wisely and to quickly adapt if you are striking out. If you go knocking at 10 a.m. every day and you never connect with anyone, maybe you are going at the wrong time. Consider going at 5:30 or 6:30 pm when your targets/neighbors are getting ready for dinner or right after dinner. Times when people might already be outside and half the neighborhood is going to be out mowing their lawns, getting things ready, and doing yard work are also great times to choose. Finding the right time is going to make your job a lot easier.

One insurance agent I know actually goes door knocking without actually going door to door. His strategy is to help his 6-year-old son set up a lemonade stand in their own driveway. They have a small sign that says "25 cent Lemonade and Insurance Advice." Dad stands with the kid and anytime a neighbor or passerby walks up, they get their lemonade (often comped by dad if the jogger has no change). Does the kid make a fortune? No. But it is good quality time punctuated by conversations with new and old neighbors. What's the ROI on this you might ask? Assume in an hour or 2 the dad can have 10 conversations and over the course of the time they are out there, 25 people walk by and see the sign. The neighborly branding and awareness is valuable on its own, the quality time with father is son also has value. When asked, the insurance agent told me that he has 3-4 sales a year that he can directly attribute to conversations that started at his son's lemonade stand.

More Tangible Farming Mailers

The types of mailers that you can do are pretty much limitless, but one of the better options we have seen over the years is a magnet. And again, this sounds very low tech, but when someone gets a magnet with local information on it, they never throw it away. Before we go through a few magnet ideas, I want to put out one important caveat: magnets only work if there is somewhere central like a refrigerator where clients can stick them. Most higher end and newer houses use stainless steel refrigerators that magnets may not stick to. Additionally, the use of magnets on central places declines as income/affluence increases. There are definitely exceptions to the rule but consider your audience carefully before investing too heavily in this tactic.

If you do decide to do a magnet, some content that we have seen work well and have a long shelf life is what I would call the "Important Local" magnet. These types of magnets would contain names and phone numbers on a short list for important local services:

- **Pizza or Popular Food Delivery**
- **Poison Control Number**
- **HVAC Emergency Contact**
- **Local Schools Main Office #'s**
- **Emergency Plumber**
- **Local Handyman**
- **Best Realtor Ever**
- **Children's Hospital**
- **Etc...**

The key here is to include "important" numbers so that when homeowners think about throwing it away, they will realize that these are all numbers they might need in crisis situations where they might not even have time to sift through Google for the best reviewed "Children's Hospital" etc. A parent, for instance, might want to have poison control's number ready without the aid of technology because kids will shove anything in their mouths. I hope my kid does not, but I remember putting berries into my mouth that I found in a random bush when I was a kid, and I assume kids still do things like that. Trust me, I know that anyone with a smartphone could Google these things in about 30 seconds, but having them all in the same place in a central location can be valuable to parents and those who don't want to search and compare in times of crisis (including a late night hankering for the best local pizza).

Your magnets do not have to be expensive. There are a lot of sites online where you can get them for 50 cents a piece or less. There are even bulk ordering websites[18] where you can get them and other materials even cheaper if you order in high

---

[18] www.alibaba.com — As of 2018 Alibaba is one of the world's biggest online retailers with sales surpassing both Amazon and Ebay.

quantities. To further get the price down you may even decide to partner with some of the local businesses that you feature to help share the cost.

As with the other letters we discussed, the other main factor is choosing who to send/give the magnets to. A good start is the neighborhood you live in, where you can anticipate the best and most useful businesses to include. Second best will likely be past clients in a certain radius, this is especially helpful for existing and tenured sales people who have done well in a certain area or city over time and have some level of familiarity. Depending on your market saturation and your budget, it can also make sense to take these areas where you have many past clients and farm their neighbors as well. Don't have past clients? Don't live in a neighborhood? No problem. A clever magnet or mailer can still get your name in front of your farm in the area of your choice. Just see the earlier chapter on choosing a farm.

Ending Tangible Farming On a High Note — An Oldie But A Goodie

As we discussed in previous chapters, mailers work best when the information they contain is either funny or valuable. When it comes to value, getting someone an accurate home value, especially in an up market, can be a great place to start. Choose a few neighborhoods that you think have had especially good value appreciation over the last 2 years and begin to send out quarterly mailers with home values. Kind of like a neighborhood update.

I remember that a Realtor in my parent's neighborhood would send out a regular quarterly neighborhood newsletter that focused on values and home sales. It would include any home that listed or sold with the bedrooms, bathrooms, square footage, price, and occasionally fun facts if she knew the families or houses well. She mailed this out to a 1200 home area for over 15 years. Not surprisingly, even though she didn't often update her photo on her mailers or signs, she consistently got new listings and sales in that same area. It became one of those mailers that people requested if they missed it. Mailers like this get opened not only by people who want to know how their house stacks up, but also by nosey neighbors. These "nosey neighbors" are often the ones you want to get your branding in front of most because they are the loudest and most talkative in each neighborhood.

PRO TIP: *If you are already planning on putting the time in to pull this data, you may as well also repurpose the home stats on Facebook and other online or email marketing options. You can do YouTube videos. You can do Facebook videos. You can post this information to apps like Nextdoor. Once you have the data, put it everywhere. You have already done the hard work, and you never know which medium a would be client may respond best to.*

BUYERS & SELLERS AS AMMUNITION

Reiterating A Crazy Important Concept

In the above chapters on farming, we briefly touched on the buyer/seller letter as ammo and what it should say, but the overall concept of using what you have (e.g. buyers or listings) in order to get what you want is such an important concept that it deserves a deeper discussion. I can't stress enough that if you get into the mentality of using every asset you have to prospect for more business, you will consistently grow your bottom line and total sales without having to pay your hard earned money to online lead sites and other costly and un-fun forms of marketing.

I have never been a hunter, but the overall idea of hunting and fishing makes a lot of sense to me. The more ammunition or bait you have, the more opportunity you have to catch something. I think this is a universal truth that we can all pretty much understand and real estate operates no differently.

If you want to get busier, the fastest way to do it is to be busy in the first place. Now I know that statement may seem redundant, a bit insulting, and not at all helpful, but it's a fact. The key is to make yourself busy with tasks and activities that either get you around people or are business related. Immerse yourself in the clients you do have and go above and beyond. It's almost like that week before you take a vacation; it is always the busiest week ever. If you want to get busy, start planning a vacation ASAP. The snowball effect is very real in real estate sales. Being busy helps you get busier. Each subsequent client you pick up, in essence, becomes a lure to get the next one, and so on. The snowball grows into an avalanche.

When we are talking about having more ammunition/bait/lures etc., one of the ways to do this is to really make the most out of it every single client/lead/name that you have. The idea here is that every single buyer that you have who is looking for a house is ammunition to prospect for more listings, and every single client you have that is listing their house is ammunition to pick up new buyers. Every person on earth has wants and needs of some kind. The key for turning these into sales is to take a list of wants and needs and turn them into tangible opportunities for others.

This overall concept of an opportunity as ammunition is most easily and classically illustrated if you think about the listing side of a transaction, because every time you get a listing you, in essence, are getting a (hopefully) shiny new object to market (your ammunition).

We have talked more about Realtors than lenders thus far, but here specifically lenders have a big opportunity because they have lists of pre-approved buyers and hopefully a clear understanding of their client's budgets and location preferences. This info can be extremely useful when shared with Realtor partners who need to put a quick deal together for customers who wants to sell quick. Similarly, there are opportunities to connect your buyers who have lost out multiple times, with houses that your Realtors have listed that have been sitting on the market for a while

Ammunition From A Listing

- For sale sign in the yard with your info
- Sharing it to social media
- Various website links generated by the MLS and your brokerage featuring the house, and you as the listing agent. (These work best as ammunition if you receive the lead when someone requests info.)
- Opportunity to host open houses and meet buyers
- Opportunity to door knock the neighborhood to let them know their neighbor is selling
- Opportunity to door knock neighborhood to let them know home sold, and to let them know if you still have buyers looking.
- Opportunity to send notes to neighbors offering home values etc.
- Hundreds of others...

Do you get the picture? Each listing is an endless supply of ammunition to pick up buyers and more listings. All you have to do is pull the proverbial trigger by applying tangible action in the form of some of the above opportunities.

Don't have many listings to use as ammunition but still want to play the game? You are not alone. At the time of this writing (2019) many real estate sales people around the country are short on listings because of an almost nationwide inventory shortage. Inventory is at all time lows in many areas. Six years ago it was the complete opposite. The good news is that low inventory can be ammunition for a high opportunity in the hands of savvy sales professionals. When supply (inventory) is low, demand (buyers) is high. You can use you can use your buyer's needs to coax curious sellers out of the wings and get them thinking more seriously by presenting them with a tangible offer or scenario.

Here is the idea. When you present someone with a tangible amount of money in exchange for their house, the chance that they are going to give your proposal a chance goes up tenfold. Compare this to how other sales people market with cold calls and door knocks to simply tell them that if they wanted to sell/buy you could help. They aren't thinking about selling their house so your message isn't going to break through to them. What I like to do is take your buyers and create a profile of them that you can tangibly present to potential sellers.

For Example:
John and Susie are two people moving from X city. They are pre-approved with X mortgage company. They are ready to go. They really want to be in your neighborhood, but they can not find anything for sale. Would you consider letting them walk through your house?

If you were to take every buyer you have, create a profile and a wants list for them, and then tangibly market this to the areas/homes they are looking for, you would create new opportunities for yourself every single time, thus using your buyers to multiply your listings. Not only that, but your effort will be seen by your buyers and be appreciated, thus leading to happier customers and likely better referral sources.

Marketing with real buyers as examples is a lot more effective than simply going door knocking saying, "Hey, I am a Realtor. You should sell your house with me because the market is hot." This is not a very tangible concept that a stranger can grasp onto. The real estate process is so personal, and it is so emotional that people would rather sell to "someone" than just sell for the sake of selling. Plus, sellers don't like the uncertainty of not knowing how long their home will take to sell on the open market. The opportunity to sell to specific buyers, for a specific amount of money, possibly closing on a specific end date, makes the deal tangible and increases everybody's chances of success.

The Double Bonus

Not only will this strategy of using buyers/sellers as ammunition help you to hopefully pick up more listings and overall business, but it can also help greatly in an even more important way. It will help you both add to, and demonstrate, the value your bring to your buyers and sellers. Think about it. What are you really doing as a Realtor for your buyers? Of course, you are showing them houses. Of course, you are "getting" them access to the MLS. But especially for those picky buyers who are not finding houses quickly, they may not see your value as fast as you think they should. You are going to be doing a lot of negotiation for them down the road, and eventually, you are going to get them through inspections, appraisal, and the lending process. You are going to be doing all these other things, but until they find the right home, nothing matters. Thus, anything you can do to show them your value, before the stage where they find a home, is crucial. And if you are using sellers as ammunition and door knocking/calling/marketing with their specific case in mind, you are truly working for them. Since many agents may rely on the MLS to find the home, if you go out of your way and explain your value to your clients, that is measurable added value.

If you have sellers instead of buyers, the concept still works the same way. What can you do to go above and beyond in market the home using your sellers listing itself as ammunition? How can you then show this above and beyond tangible marketing you are doing to your sellers so they realize you are doing more than getting their property on the web?

If You Want To Use The Ammo Strategy, But Don't Have Any Ammo Yet

A common question I get all the time when I talk about this strategy is "What do you do if you don't have any listings or buyers to use as ammo?" Maybe you are brand new to sales or you just relocated to a new city. How can you possibly use this strategy if you don't have anything going on, no ammunition to fire? Here is the good news, most sales people don't use their ammunition to even 50% of its potential, so there is plenty to borrow. So really, if you are new to the business or new to the area, you can get started by connecting with other agents within your marketplace or within your own office. Of all of the crazy new technologies and bells and whistles that each office brags about, being able to use your co-worker's existing productivity to help get your ball rolling is a major tangible asset of working at a company that many people overlook.

I can almost guarantee that of the top 10 busiest agents in your office or your marketplace, only a small portion, if any, are fully utilizing each buyer and listing as ammunition to pick up more. This is your opportunity. They are probably not sending out 50-60 letters prospecting on behalf of every single buyer they have. They are not door knocking for each client either. They simply don't have the time. So for these people, why not team up with them and just say, "Hey, let's meet up once a week. If you give me an updated list of all of your buyer and seller needs. I will door knock, make calls, and send letters to help find the right house or buyer for each of your clients respectively."

Unless you are talking to a big team that is overstaffed and looking for ways to keep their team members busy, you are likely presenting a win-win situation. It is not going to cost the other sales person anything. If you find them a house or a buyer, you only get one side of the deal and they will still get the side they were likely going to get anyway. You can now use not only what you have as ammunition, but what your colleagues and coworkers have as well, to stay busy and keep the proverbial snowball growing at all times. And as long as there is demand in the real estate market, there should be activity in your pipeline.

PRO TIP: *If your office, team, or local real estate board has a Facebook group, check it out! People are constantly posting needs. Someone is looking for a house for next year. Someone's looking for a rental. Someone else needs a home with an in-law suite. When someone presents you with the demand, they have already done half the work for you by providing the ammo. Remember to get creative.*

Looking for Demand Digitally

Starting with your internal office groups on Facebook and other social media platforms is a great first step, but there are so many other places where people post what they are looking for online. Where most sales people use social media to "shout," this strategy actually recommends using social media to listen. Simply check out apps like NextDoor as well as various Facebook groups in your community, and listen to what people are asking for. Often times real estate needs do pop up. These needs become your demand, and once you know what they need, you can initiate a conversation and then find them what they are looking for. On the same token, it is okay to post every once and a while about what you are looking for. The key here, similar to the main premise of the book overall is to be specific. Don't tell the general public and your core audience online that you are looking for buyers and sellers. Let them know the specific type of buyer or seller that you are looking for. Be a connector amongst your various audiences both digitally and in real life.

BEING A CONNECTOR

What Is A Connector

Being a connector is not specifically just about real estate and lead generation. I would call this a philosophy on life. Although each of us are all connectors to some degree, those who make it a focus tend to build social capital that translates into success in all areas of life and business. To understand how to be a better connector, and how to make it pay off we should first explore what a connector is.

A "connector" is someone who goes out of their way to connect their friends with their colleagues, to connect their colleagues with their friends, and to make sure that if someone out there is looking for a referral that they are the ones who are going making that referral happen. Connectors collect relationships and find value in all of the people they meet. They try to better understand the connection types people are looking for, and are in tune with the needs of everyone they meet with by the end of a conversation. Connectors don't usually make money off of getting person A connected to person B, but rather they trade in and grow assets that are much more valuable: social capital and top of mind status.

Connectors Stay Top Of Mind[19]

If you are the person who is constantly giving someone else referrals to people they can connect with, you are a part of the reason that they can feed their kids. You are a part of the reason that they can send their oldest to college next year. You are a time saver for them because your connection meant they didn't have to search for a solution themselves.

When you are a connector, you matter, and you are always top of mind. Whatever business you are in, whether it is real estate, mortgages, marketing or something else, if you can be a connector, in addition to being good at your job and being trustworthy, your business will grow as a result of the social capital you accrue. This social capital will result in you being a go-to-person for more than just what you sell. For instance, I "sell" marketing consultations. Sure, I want to be the go-to person for any Realtor looking for marketing ideas, but by developing connections within my network, I can become the top of mind contact for many other topics as

---

[19] Top of Mind Concept — When someone thinks of your industry, product or service, they think of you. When real estate pops up in a conversation, a customer immediately thinks of you.

well. This helps to get my phone ringing. As a sales person who hates to cold call, any time my phone rings, it's a good thing.

The biggest change in my life over the last 10 years has really just been realizing that there is an opportunity to make referrals hundreds of times per day. I would never want to be in a position where I did not have someone trustworthy to recommend. Whenever someone asks for something and I can't offer a solution I feel like I've missed a huge opportunity, and I think "Hey! I need to meet and develop a relationship with a person who does that, and add them to my list for the next time someone needs that respective good or service."

I'm a member of Facebook groups that have become hotbeds of activity for finding opportunities to be a connector. Neighbors and friends are constantly posting looking for connections. The ones I see most often are people looking for contractors, babysitters, plumbers, and electricians. The other big ask that I often see is restaurant recommendations for specific situations. This was part of the reason I became super active with Yelp and Instagram. Not only do I love going out to eat, but I also love connecting people to new restaurants and dishes. Again, being a connector gets you top of mind, and being top of mind for any topic gets you more at-bats for your desired topic or product.

Being a connector has been a natural fit for me. The more that I am able to connect my colleagues with my friends and vice versa, the more I am able to create new meaningful relationships and be able to always stay top of mind.

Another benefit of being a connector is the theory of reciprocity. Even though you are giving someone a connection and not a direct sale, you are increasing the chance that the person you helped will want to help you back. The key here is to let people know how they can help you. Honesty and directness are big assets here. If people know how to help you, they will. Make sure that if people seem to be fans and are connecting you to others, that you tell them if the connections end up being good. I wouldn't tell someone that a connection was "terrible," but letting people know who you were and were not able to work with is a way to improve the quality of the connections or "leads" they give you.

The people in the world who are the biggest connectors have the most social capital. It always seems like their businesses grow faster than everybody else's. Realtors, and lenders, in particular, are likely more suited to be connectors than any other profession out there. Think about it: if you are a Realtor, you know lenders, you know title people, you know insurance people, you know investors, you know people with the city, you know local business owners, you know so many different people, and not to mention the 3,000 other agents in town who are your colleagues. In addition, you know referral sources for almost anything a home buyer or seller could need:

- Stagers
- Photographers
- House Cleaners
- Lawn Services
- Handymen
- Plumbers
- Roofers
- Contractors/Remodelers
- Builders
- Electricians
- HVAC Companies
- Painters
- Movers
- Interior Designers
- Architects
- Furniture Sales
- Tree Removal Services
- Gutter Cleaners
- Pool Help
- **Snow Removal (if you are in a frigid state like me)**

The list goes on. What others can you add to this list? Real estate professionals are in a prime position to give referrals out for a whole host of different services and thus those people are going to be more poised to give referrals back to you. If you had 20 types of professionals you developed relationships with, and to whom you actively tried to refer business, wouldn't it stand a chance that you would receive either leads in return or at least a bigger network? The bigger network, whether or not direct leads follow, also becomes the base for added social capital that in the end will amplify your prospecting attempts.

The idea is pretty simple: give as many referrals as you can. Stalk every Facebook group you can. Stalk every LinkedIn group. Whenever someone asks for a referral for anything, find one. Even if it is not directly someone in your immediate network. Find someone who did good by one of your friends and refer that person out. Say, "Hey, I referred you to "Contractor X". I have not used them personally, but my brother used him and he was fantastic." Not only is giving the referral the key component to getting more, but giving a good referral is critical. Now what I mean by a good referral is not only are you sending someone's information to another party. You are also calling the other party to let them know that they might be expecting your call and possibly going the extra mile and giving that other person's information out. If I'm referring a contractor to a Realtor, I will usually screenshot the contractor's information, send it to the Realtor and then I will send the contractor an email or phone call and let them know that I sent their name to "X Realtor" and give the contact with the Realtor's number so that they can reach out directly if they want to. That way everyone knows that I'm trying to help them and can also suggest if there is a better way to refer/recommend them.

I truly look at giving referrals and being a connector as a win-win strategy, because not only do you naturally grow your network, social capital, and list of people who like you, but you are also genuinely helping others. Aside from the profits we all make when we close a deal as a result of a referral there is also the intrinsic value you gain from simply knowing that you helped someone else out.

The whole process of being a connector comes naturally to some but not to others. Often it is hardest for people who haven't worked in a referral centric industry before. If you fall into this group, or you just want to get more strategic about your connector activities, I recommend building two data sets. The first would be in your contact list (spreadsheet). You would simply add a column for each contact where you enter types of people and services you could refer to each client.

For Example:
You are out showing houses or taking a new loan application from John. John happens to be an electrician who works at a local pool/spa store. He coordinates and manages the electrical installation of new pools and hot tubs. You ask if sending him buyers who were thinking about buying or installing a hot tub/pool might be helpful. He lets you know that it would be great because he, in fact, gets bonuses based on

bringing in new business and also earns opportunities for overtime the more work he has. You make a quick note, and once he leaves, you go into your contact list and update John's column on "how to help him" and add that anytime someone mentions that they are thinking about a pool or hot tub, John is your guy. You take it a step further and email him the next day to let him know you appreciate him telling you that because you always love having an expert to go to for your client's needs.

The second type of data to compile is a checklist of types of businesses you could refer to your clients for them to use. You can take the above list, and add other business types to it (adding more every time you learn more about your clients). Then as you are in meetings with clients simply go through the checklist with them and see who they might want information for. Since many are home related, giving them the whole list at the end might be a great option. Many agents already do this, but taking it one step further by going through it verbally with clients does two extra things. First, it shows your client that you are looking out for their current and future needs, as well as shows them that you are well connected. Second, an in-person conversation increases the chances they will remember your offer of connections.

PRO TIP: *Many sales people track the leads they receive and sort them by lead source (something we already discussed earlier in the book) but the second dimension of this that fits in great if you are a connector, is to track referrals received as well. If you have 20 service professionals on your list that you refer out, can you track how many referrals you received from each one of them? It sets up a great opportunity to do end of year or even quarterly follow-ups, to not only stay in front of them, but to say thank you and to communicate graciously to ensure that they feel appreciated. If you are sending someone a lot but you never hear from them, check in to make sure you are referring them the right way and that they want you to keep referring them. Similarly, if you haven't heard from them in a while it can be good to reconnect, see how things are going, and remind them of the type of people you like to connect with.*

Being A Connector Outside Of Business

Being a connector isn't just for helping people in one business to connect with people who can be colleagues or customers with the intent of their being money exchanged or services provided. This concept works socially as well. When people move to a new area, they often need and like to meet new people, not to make money and grow their referral network, but simply to have friends both for themselves and their kids. I have seen real estate sales people who have truly helped their clients not only to buy homes but to introduce them to other clients, friends, and neighbors. When someone is new to an area, developing those first few relationships is critical because it helps people to get assimilated and grounded into their new communities. If you are at the center of their first relationships or friend circles, the chances are higher that you will remain a part of their lives. You will get invited to more parties, get more Christmas cards, and overall be around without having to send salesy postcards or having to make constant prospecting calls. The best way to grow your own network of good friends and acquaintances is to help others to grow theirs.

One of my best friends is an agent and at least 4-5 times per year he has us over for dinner or drinks to introduce us to some new clients of his who just moved here from out of town who have something in common with us. He thinks we will get along and wants them to have friends in the area. He usually hits the nail on the head, and we almost always love the people he introduces us to, many of whom are now themselves close friends for both my wife, me, and our son. Not only has this agent put himself in multiple friend circles in our lives, but he has also become a more meaningful part of his client's moving process. A house is only an asset made of bricks/wood/materials. A house is what most buyers are physically looking for, but being a part of a community and developing new relationships makes a house a home.

Make a checklist of questions to ask your clients that can prompt the referral process. The below are just examples of common referral sources for real estate professionals, the ones mentioned earlier in this chapter can be added or swapped in depending on who you know!

- **Do you have a tax preparer?**
- **Do you have a financial adviser?**
- **Do you have a lender/Realtor?**
- **Do you have a title person?**
- **Do you have an insurance agent?**
- **Do you have a plumber a handyman?**
- **Do you have a lawn service?**

Because giving and receiving referrals is the bedrock of most successful sales based businesses I wanted to go deeper here. The next chapter is by Josh Smith, one of the people I respect most in the real estate industry. Among my circles, we jokingly refer to him as "the voice of reason" for his ability to break down even the most complex topics into tangible and easily digestible pieces of advice.

THE POWER OF A STRONG REFERRAL

GUEST WRITTEN BY JOSH SMITH

Josh Smith is an entrepreneur, business owner, and high-level advisor. On a daily basis, he actively leads his company and advises many successful business owners, contractors, real estate investors, and high-level salespeople. He is the Co-Founder & Managing Partner at The Fulton Group, a $25 million real estate holding company. He is also the Founder of The Front Porch Group a nationally recognized remodeling company that found their niche in asking real estate agents and mortgage lenders for hard referrals, for real projects.

The Realization

When we are asked where our business comes from, I would guess that most of us would say: referrals. I would go so far as to wager that most of us would say that more than 80% of our business regularly comes from referrals. Good sales people and good business owners design their business this way on purpose.

We work and live in a referral society. Referrals are the life-blood of our business in many cases. They are extremely important and worth a ton to us. Moreover, the referral partners—those who refer customers to us—are even more coveted.

Referral partners are one of the most powerful assets any sales person or business owner can leverage for huge growth. Creating a network of strong referral partners is one of the key ingredients that you will find when dissecting any playbook of a person at the top of their field.

A lot of our businesses are built from referrals because it is a fantastic way to create longevity in the business for a very low cost. It typically provides the highest return on investment to go deep in relationships and have your referral partners refer you business, often times a higher return on investment than any other marketing effort.

I think we can all agree, referrals are huge and can make or break us in sales and business. But do we really have a full understanding of just why that is?

A Deeper Understanding Of Why

Sure, there are all the normal reasons that we think of right away to explain why referrals are great for us, all the reasons we all believe from above. But the real reason is how much easier, streamlined, and less stressful it makes our day to day workflow, that is, our processes and systems that make us efficient.

Referrals are not about cost savings in dollars, they are about cost savings in your time, your effort, and your energy! It's about the upside potential that you create for yourself by having referral partners that know, like, and trust you and who convey that to the customer who calls you, and therefore makes your job simpler!

Think about the last lead that you paid for, whether it was a call from a billboard ad you bought, an email off a mailer, or online lead. Think about the lack of trust you initially had with that cold lead. Think about the number of objections you needed to overcome. Think about the skepticism the prospect had. Think about the price objections you heard. Think about the extra amount of thought and conversation you needed to have to make that sale.

Now, on the other hand, think about the last lead that was referred to you. Think about how much smoother that transaction went. Think about how there was likely already some knowledge and trust assumed when they called you. Think about how much easier it was to build rapport. Think about how the pricing did not matter as much. Think about how much more fun it was to talk with this customer.

Where do you want to compete every day? I want to compete where the commission check comes easier and with more enjoyment.

Why We Often Lose Sight

Once we truly have an understanding of the real reason "why" referrals are more valuable than any other type of lead, then we need to understand why sometimes we lose sight of this gold mine we have right in front of us.

There are usually two reasons:

1. Getting referrals does not have the awesome "wow" factor, it's not shiny and new, and it's not an overly tangible item to see in the exact moment.
2. We don't have a good tangible system and process to constantly leverage our referral partner relationships and add value to them.

We need to have an understanding that it takes work, specifically hard work, to cultivate our referral partner relationships. It always takes time. There are no shortcuts to developing great relationships. Relationships are started in a moment but developed over a very long period of time.

We need to have commitment to a system and process that is going to ensure that we keep a constant eye on that which is the lifeblood of our business. This system does not need to be complicated. We just need to have it and commit to making sure we follow and follow up on it on a daily, weekly, monthly basis.

Three Common Misconceptions & The Solutions

Giving and getting referrals the correct way is going to ensure that you set yourself and your referral partners up for the highest probability of success. These are the 3 most common misconceptions about referrals that, if you can master, will further your ability to leverage the most precious source of business we all have.

Misconception #1: People know how to refer me, they just give out my name and number and tell people to call me.

We are making a big mistake and missing out in enormous proportion if we think that just by asking our referral partners to give out our name and number that we will receive quality referrals. Did you learn to ride a bike just by someone saying "Please go ride a bike."? No, absolutely not. We needed someone there to give us an idea of how to do it, coaching, tips, instruction, reminders, and suggestions on how to ride a bike. We needed encouragement to get back on once we fell off.

It was not easy and did not come naturally to us until we had instruction. Referrals are no different than learning to ride a bike or any other task we do ourselves or tasks we give to others.

The Solution: Teach your partners how to refer you.

We want to make the strongest referral possible when giving a referral and we want to receive strong referrals from our partners as well. If our partners believe in us and we believe in our partners, it's a natural desire for quality referrals to be given successfully on all fronts.

There is a very simple and tangible way to have an open and honest dialogue about how we can give and get better referrals. Here is how it goes: Go meet with all your current referral partners and say a version of this: "Thanks so much for referring Sally to me last week! Hey, question, what do you want me to say about you to build you up when one of the people you refer to me calls?" Let your partner tell you 3 big things that make them stand out and are important to them and then whenever you get a call from someone they refer to you, say those things about that referral partner! It is simple and easy and it builds up and adds credibility to your partner with that client. Why? Because you are a professional and are saying 3 great and tangible things about them that reassures the customer that they themselves know and are working with smart people.

After you talk about how you can talk them up, say this back to your referral partner: "Can I please tell you the 3 most important things I want you to say when you make a referral to me?" Their answer will always be "Yes, sure, I would love that. What do you want me to tell clients about you?"

Give your referral partner 3 tangible things that are important for any customer to know about you which will give you a position of strength when they call you.

Figure out what your 3 things are. Here are some examples:

1. I am constantly in the top 5 for customer service in the annual area rankings.

2. I have been in the business for over 30 years and served over 5,000 customers.

3. I take pride in making sure my customers always are over communicated too.

If you do this right now with all of your referral partners AND have this same conversation at least 2x per year as a "reminder", you will see the number of quality referrals you receive go through the roof. More importantly, you will more easily land the customer, increase your lead to closing ratio, and have more fun doing it!

Misconception #2: If I am referred a name and number to call — that's great!

Getting a name and number given to you from your referral partner that you need to then reach out to is NOT great. At the surface level, you would ask: "Why not? That's great! It's a lead from a referral partner for goodness sake."

Solution: Create a business of incoming calls.

What you want to do is to get the customers to call you. Why? Several reasons. They are interrupting you when they call you vs. you interrupting them at some weird or bad time for them. They know who they are calling vs. you having to explain who you are. If they initiate the call they know why they are reaching out vs. them not knowing why you are calling right away.

All of those items create a position of strength from the get-go and put you in a position of professionalism. You are the professional. The customer wants and needs a service from you. There is something else too, if they were referred the right way and they call you, you know they are serious and they need something from you if they are calling, not you needing something from them.

I understand that these are subtleties, but they are crucially important. Build your business on incoming calls, not outgoing calls! This will lead to more enjoyment for both you and your customers.

Misconception #3: It's okay for me to be referred with 2 other service providers.

It is not okay for your name to be "thrown in the ring" amongst a total of 3 people by your referral partners. Why? Because it's a weak referral, and we do not build wildly successful businesses from weak referrals! It's a recipe for disaster, headaches, heartaches, and simply not the way optimal to do business on either side of the table.

When your referral partner refers you out with others they are painting themselves as less sure in a transaction where customers need ultimate confidence. On your end, when you are referred to in a group you go from being a sought after professional to a run of the mill commodity.

The Solution: One and only one.

Your referral partner is not doing themselves, the customer, or you any service by referring more than one person for one specific service. I do not care if my referral partner does not want to refer me in a specific deal or to a specific customer; however, I ask that when they do refer me, they referred me and only me. If they can't do that, then I am not doing my job to show and prove that I am the best fit for their customers. And if that's the case, I would rather keep working on that than working on winning deals where I am referred to as a commodity.

Looks at it this way: if someone is new to your town and bumped into you on the street and asks you, "Hey where is the best burger joint in this town?" Are you going to reply: "Well, you could go to Joe's Burger Joint, or you could go to Billy's Burger Joint, or you could go to Sally's Burger Joint, they're all pretty good."

You wouldn't do that! That would just confuse the out-of-town visitor. What you would do is think a minute and say something like: "You really should go to Sally's Burger Joint. They are right around the corner, their burgers are fantastic, their service is great, their atmosphere is awesome, and they have the best french fries too".

If that's how we would refer someone to find a burger, why wouldn't we do the same thing for much bigger and more expensive transaction referrals? Would we really refer someone in a stronger way to a $5 burger joint than we would for a $200,000 transaction? That just does not make any sense.

People are seeking advice from you, give it to them! There is so much noise in this world; what people are seeking and need is some straight, honest, and simple advice.

Ask Yourself

Are you taking it to the next level in this part of your business? Are you coaching your referral partners on how to refer you? Are you adding value to your partners by building them up to the customer when they call you?

If we agree that referrals are so strong, then we should spend time meeting, developing relationships with, and coaching our referral partners on how to refer us, what to say about us, and making sure we are always loving on our referral partners with honor.

To make a tangible difference in your business, you must realize the tremendous value in referrals, put a system in place to make sure you are leveraging your referral partners, and always remember that referrals are more profitable, more fun, and more likely to build your business for strength and longevity.

Make your referrals with passion and conviction, and ask for referrals in the same way.

EMAIL MARKETING

There is one form of marketing that I think every person should be doing. This is almost a non-negotiable if you want to meet with me and talk about how to grow your business. That form of marketing is email.

For me, email marketing is great because it's customizable, personalizable, and often cheap. When most people hear the term email marketing they immediately think of the word "spam." Email is so easy that it is easy for companies and "bad actors" to overuse, use wrong, and use without putting in any effort. All of these scenarios end with low results and consumers who become trained experts at figuring out whether they want to give you their "junk" email address or their real one. Second, they become experts at deleting emails based on the subject lines. And third, they become experts at figuring out if your first email was a waste of time, how to unsubscribe or mentally note to delete all of your future emails before opening. What I am saying here is that to make email marketing work for you, you need to offer big value. Big value that is tangible and is easy for your recipients to see.

Who To Send To

Similar to mailers, the first thing to figure out is the audience. The best group is always going to be people who you already know. Keeping in mind that the better you know someone, the more personal the email can be. This task is made easiest by categorizing your contacts into groups and sending different versions of each email to different groups.

A second type of email marketing can be to people who fit more of a B2B (business to business) agenda. For instance, emailing other agents or other lenders to see what types of deals they can't do, or to see areas they don't work in, that you do. Many of the most successful email marketing campaigns that my teams have done have been B2B. The simple fact that email is more widely used in business time than in personal time means that your email will be more likely to get opened.

A third type of email marketing is to send emails to soft leads. Think about all of the leads you have generated from all of the above strategies in this book. Did any of them not immediately buy a house from you? Did a large portion never get back with you after a few contacts? Did a Zillow or other online lead turn out to not be as motivated as you initially hoped? Email is a perfect medium to stay in touch with these people with quality information so that when they eventually do decide to get serious about home buying, you will at least still be in front of them. Many professionals whom I work with send 1-2 emails per month to their "old leads." For those with more than 250 contacts on their list we typically see 1-2 converting back into active shoppers every single month.

What To Send With

If you have more than 50 or so people on your list who you want to email, you should probably invest time, money, or both into an email marketing software. There are so many email systems out there, where should you start? Now, what this comes down to is that it really does not matter which email marketing system you use, as long as you have your database in a CSV or Excel (spreadsheet) file and you have time blocked out to update and add to your records. Any CRM system (that I have seen) will accept data from an excel file.

Choosing a CRM that works for you is important but can be confusing. Every company I visit has some different crazy CRM, and companies often change systems every couple of years based on technology, new goals, and to cast the illusion that a new system will be better. At the end of the day, we know from experience that the best systems aren't necessarily the ones that have the most bells and whistles. Rather, **the best systems are the ones that get used.** Likewise, the systems that get used are often the ones that are simplest, and that can be accessed and easily used across devices.

If you work at a medium or large company the first step that I would take is to see if the CRM your company is already providing you will be a fit for your goals/ needs. Does it seem easy to use? Does it let you simply send emails out and save notes about customers? Can you update from your phone OR your computer? What you may end up seeing is that the CRM your company provides you is clunky and does too much, making even the simplest tasks hard to accomplish. It is likely that your company designed it to meet the need of every single sales person in the world, rather than the needs of any specific person, region, or team.

As with any tool or device in your life, just because you have something that does a million things, you don't have to use every function. My oven, for instance, has 20+ buttons, however, the only ones I ever use are set heat and set time. Those two buttons accomplish my goals every time. Sure, one day I may use another feature but on that day it will be an added bonus, rather than being the hindrance of one more thing to learn when I just want to eat. **Tangible marketing is the same: it is goal-related and task specific.** Find a system that lets you accomplish your biggest goals in the simplest way possible. If the system happens to do another function that replaces a different system you have, then it's a double win. For instance, if the CRM you choose also has a mass texting function that replaces a current mass texting system you have, you may be able to condense into one system where everything is in one place and you only pay one fee.

Definitely take some time to explore any system that is available to you through the company dues you are already paying. Before you start uploading all of your data and taking weeks to get your new system set up, first write down some needs you have and then look to see if your new system accomplishes it. If the system doesn't accomplish your goals, do you really need it? Or will it end up being one more activity you have to spend time on that doesn't get you in front of prospective clients? Remember, you don't meet new leads in a CRM. Tools like CRMs exist to help you better communicate, maintain and grow the relationships and leads (new and old) that you already have.

Getting Tangible With Your CRM — Single Email Blasts

If you want a specific task that a CRM can perform to help you generate business the one I would look for is the ability to send out single mass email blasts to various groups from your contact list. Many systems make it easy to set up "set it and forget it" 12 step drip campaigns, but not easy to send out single blast emails. 12 and 20 step programs should be used to slowly recover after you hit rock bottom, not to develop relationships with high value contacts. In essence, all systems provide the ability for users to waste their time, and the time of everyone on their list, but few systems make it easy to send out clever, well worded and semi-personalized emails to small groups.

The reason I love single emails is that they are more personal, and they are slightly more timely. Plus, you can really track the results easily. With a single blast email that's not tied to a campaign, you can be nimble and agile. You can take an idea from your head to execution in minutes.

For example, in the real estate industry, interest rates change all the time. Many of my colleagues will send out mass emails to their "To Be Determined" list of prospective clients whenever something happens in the economy that may signal a change for the better or worse. People on the TBD list are those who at some point you were in contact with to help them buy a home, but for one reason or another, they haven't found a home to buy yet or haven't pulled the trigger on moving forward. The email will usually tell prospects who are on the fence that now is the time to start planning if they want to save money long term on their mortgage. The email is fairly specific to a need that we know the receivers have, the need to buy a home in the near future. The content of the email plays to the emotions of the receiver, a little bit of fear of higher bills, but also to the excitement of getting started and saving money.

When it comes to email marketing, and now a lot of other marketing as well, (think robo-calls, auto text messages, etc.) I think a lot of us get trapped in the idea that we need to "automated this" and "set and forget" that. Think about the sales people you love and the companies that you like to buy things from. Do they bombard your email with automated garbage all the time? Most likely the answer will be no. You are not selling a pair of shoes; you are selling the American Dream and yourself. The house, mortgage, or policy that you are selling is a big deal, and as such, your marketing emails need to be pertinent, specific, and above all valuable. If the first mass email you send to someone doesn't fit into the above three categories the likelihood that the receiver will never open one of your emails again goes up exponentially. This "open rate" can be measured by most systems and you can look to see what the open rates on your emails are. If you are putting people into a 12 step email campaign with generic information I would be shocked if you had an open rate above 10% by the fourth email. However, if you send an email to a list of your clients in a certain city about something going on in that city with an added blurb about home prices there, and you send a similar email on a quarterly basis I would bet you could maintain a 40% or above open rate.

If you need a system that will allow you to send out these single mass emails or small campaigns to segments of your contact list, one easy to use and a mostly free system is Mailchimp.com. I am not getting paid by MailChimp, I am just mentioning them because they are a great free beginner system. It is simple to add a list of contacts and to then send them an email. This system couldn't be any more user-friendly. It's incredibly simple and you can use it for free until you have 2,000 contacts (for most real estate professionals, 2,000 contacts is quite a few people.)

MailChimp is a great option for those who simply want to send 1 large email to 1 list of people. But there are systems that do more, or that are better for a specific goal. Follow Up Boss, for instance, is great if you buy a ton of Zillow leads and want a system that will automatically input and start working those leads. The system you choose should be the one that is the best fit for your overall business and budget. In the coming section, we will cover some general tips that have helped our clients and colleagues to generate more and better business with email marketing regardless of the exact system they chose.

Tangible Tips For Email Marketing

Tip 1: Sort By City

Send out city-specific emails. For instance, if you had an open house in Plymouth, Michigan you could choose to send that open house email specifically to the people in your database who live in Plymouth. This will increase the relevancy of your email because it is city specific. It will also increase the chances of people showing up to your open house because it is physically closer to them. These same people are also more likely to know others who also live in that city, so even if they aren't interested, the odds that they know people who are looking to buy in their city is high.

Tip 2: Personalize Emails By Always Inserting "First Name."

The reason that you want the first name field always filled out separately from the last name field in your initial CRM spreadsheet or database is that you can personalize mass communications such as emails this way. An email that starts with, "Hey John" Or, "Hey Matt" is always going to do better than the one that says, "Hey neighbor." Most people skip the "insert first name" function in their email marketing software, but it is an easy way to increase the relevance of your email with one easy click if your CRM list is set up the right way. If you are a MailChimp user the footnote here offers a simple guide to personalizing details in your mass emails with merge tags.[20] Of note, you can insert any field from your spreadsheet into a mass email using merge tags. Examples of fields you could and might want to merge into your emails include: client first name, city name, interest rate, closing anniversary date and much more.

Tip 3: Simple Emails Often Perform Better

Not everyone will agree with me here but I have seen major success rates from lenders who simply make their emails shorter and more to the point. I do not like emails that have colorful pretty borders and crazy colors with links everywhere and pictures galore. I like my email marketing like I like my coffee, plain and simple. You really want your email marketing to look like a personal email from you to someone. If you do that, your open rates will usually increase. The first time you start sending people automated newsletters and things of that nature, your open rates for almost all emails going forward are going to start tanking unless your content is amazing. Think of it this way, when people know you are sending marketing, they make a quick decision to keep paying attention or not. When the email looks like it could be personal, they will invest just a second or two more of their time to figure out what the message is all about. This is enough time to get them hooked if your messaging is short enough, offers value, or elicits curiosity.

Tip 4: Test Based on Open Rate

Whether you end up using MailChimp, your company's CRM, or any decent system from the past decade you will likely be able to see your open rate a few minutes/days after sending out your email campaign. Your open rate is the percent of people who opened your email divided by those you sent it to. A great rate is often considered over 20%.[21] If you have been sending automated newsletters and you have been sending out really long, drawn-out emails with lots of content that is not really specific to your area, check your open rate. It is probably below a couple percent. If you have been doing plain text emails that are two to three sentences long that are specific to your clients, it is not uncommon to have a 50% open rate. The better open rate is not due to the technical fact that the email was short, it is due to the content being simple. Get to the point quickly, your customers will appreciate it, and thus open more of your future emails. Those marketers receiving open rates that are higher typically have higher response rates and lead counts as well. The idea here is to tweak your subject lines, your level of personalization, your content, the days/times you send out, and anything else you can think of until your open rate gets to a level you are satisfied with.

Types Of Emails

Once you have chosen an email marketing system and you have a few tricks up your sleeve like the ones above, the next step is to figure out what emails to send out. The types of emails that you can send out are really similar to some of the letters that we already talked about. The big difference between the content you send out via email and the letters you send out is that emails will allow you to be more specific, timely, and proximate, at a fraction of the cost or time required by a traditional mailer.

Take past clients for example. If you are sending an email to past clients, you already know that they have purchased a house in the past (so you know they are homeowners, you know where they live, and that they, in theory, are familiar with you and hopefully like you). These pieces of knowledge can help you to craft any of the below types of topics into short and personalized email marketing blasts.

- **An offer to do a Comparative Market Analysis (CMA)**

- **A check in to see how your past clients are doing. Shockingly yes, a friendly email can go a long way.**

- **An invite to an event such as a client appreciation party, holiday event, or happy hour.**

- **A clever email asking for referrals to people they know.**
  Example:
  "Hey Name, There is a network of neurons in each of our brains called the reticular activator network, it helps us remember things. For instance, when you buy a new white car, you notice everyone else who also has a new white car. Realistically the same percentage of people have a white car today than last year, but you are more primed to notice because of your reticular activator after purchasing one yourself. Since you just went through the home buying process, I figured your reticular activator might know some others who are about to buy or sell homes as well. I would love to get connected to anyone you do know so I can give them the same level of service I gave you. Let me know anyone you think I should connect with. Thanks in advance and hope you are loving your new home."

- **An email with a list of homes for sale near them so they can stay on top of local real estate trends.**

- **A guide you curate to exciting local happenings in their area.**

The above all make sense and have worked for my colleagues when craftily sent to past clients and other close personal relationships. The content and frequency should of course change if the people you are sending to do not have a relationship with you. For instance, if you are sending an email to random buyer leads that never went anywhere, I am actually pretty okay with using more automated campaigns. The marketing you send out to them, really only matters if it works. And so, having something in front of them regularly is a lot is better than not a lot because they have not become customers yet. Although you still want to craft intelligent emails that offer value, the frequency with which you send these emails becomes more important. The potential targets who are going to be attracted to your email marketing are really the only ones that you care about. Sure, automated messages may turn some of these people away, and you will even have some (or even many) unsubscribe, but at the end of the day you will likely convert a percentage of these cold leads into real sales.

Regardless of whether you are marketing to warm past clients, or cold leads the content you send out is the what, and the list you send to is the who. Figure out what you are going to send to who, and "who" will likely respond to "what" and the puzzle of how to do good email marketing is solved.

Tangible Emails To Send Out

You bought this book to learn specifics. What are a couple of different emails that you can actually send out? One email that works remarkably well for many is one we call the financial advisor email.

The rationale: It's kind of an interesting fact that in the U.S., financial advisors are required to send their clients a quarterly estimate of what their assets are worth.

For most people under 40, a home is their biggest asset, often worth more than the money they have invested with their financial advisors. Even such, Realtors are not legally required to send a quarterly estimate of what your home is worth every quarter or even year. Legal requirements aside, this is a huge opportunity. We know people care about how much money they are worth and Realtors are constantly trying to find ways to stay top of mind with real value. Sending out the financial advisor letter serves both the client with the value they want and gives agents the opportunity they need.

Here is one version of the email:

> Hey [name],
>
> Hope you are doing well. My financial advisor sends me a quarterly statement of what my assets are worth and how they changed that quarter with the market. It made me think, why doesn't someone send this out for home values since there is often more total value in someone's house than in their investment account.
>
> Every year I am going to be sending out a quick CMA (comparative market analysis) with an updated value on your home.
>
> Just respond to this email with any recent updates you have done to your home. I will factor them into my report.
>
> Talk soon,
> [your name]
>
> P.S. If you have friends or family who need the same service, just let me know!

The last sentence, asking the receiver for the updates they have done to their homes is crucial because everybody likes to brag about the work they have done in their house and it is an easy question for them to answer. Someone might not even want the CMA but they may still want to brag to you. After all the real aim of the email is to spur engagement with your database. Whether they want the CMA or just want to brag to you for a moment about the updates they have done, it's a win for you. Although this type of email is most commonly sent by Realtors, lenders often send it out as well as a way to not only stay in touch but also as a means of reminding people how much equity they could be sitting on in order to help them to do cash-out refinances or to use other financial products. Additionally, it can be a good tool for lenders to use in order to pass the CMA opportunity back on to the original Realtor who sent them the deal, or as a way to connect them to a new Realtor.

A similar spin on the financial advisor email is to send a mass email with a more general positive update. The email of positivity is just letting your database know something awesome, because everybody likes opening their email to good news, especially during the work week. If every email you send has good news people will become programmed to open your emails from the chemicals in their brain that fire when positive stimuli are introduced. I would add a clever footnote here explaining this, but let's face it I work in real estate not science. Below is a short list of examples of positive email content types that we have seen agents and lenders successfully use via email marketing.

Home Prices Are Up "X" Percent
This email provides a quick and true statistic of how much home sales are up or down in a certain geographic area in a certain time frame. This is typically followed by an offer to give them a more exact value on their home specifically.

Interest Rates are Lower
Since interest rates fluctuate constantly you can pick a day or week when they happen to be a little lower than the monthly average and email your database about the great opportunity that creates.

New or Existing Loan Opportunities
Loan programs, details and limits are constantly changing and being added. Take a new or existing mortgage program and update your audience with how they or someone they know could use it to take advantage of whatever detail makes that program advantageous.

Local Developments
This email would provide a list of the 5 or 10 newest building developments or businesses coming to your area. Since new developments often affect housing prices this is usually info people want to see. Plus people always love "top" 5 or 10 lists.

Events
People are always looking for things to do and you can be there a go-to source for events and happenings in their area. Curate a list of upcoming events in your area and send it out with a frequency that makes sense for you. If your team does events of their own such as client appreciation parties or holiday events, these are also okay to send out via email.

The Anatomy Of An Email

Email Subject Line:
When you are email marketing the most important thing is actually not what your emails says in the body, it's your subject line. If you have a good (or intriguing) subject line, your email will get opened a lot more, and if it gets opened more you will get more responses. A subject line is actually shockingly like an envelope. If you have crap on the outside of an envelope that you are mailing, and it says something spammy no one is going to open it. Your subject line is essentially communicating in the same way. Keep them short, keep them simple, and make the alluring. A couple of subject lines that my team has seen work remarkably well for agents and lenders are:

- Following up
- In case you missed it
- Wanted to let you know
- Referral (because who doesn't want a referral)
- Big changes this week
- List of homes under "x" price (x being a price that would be considered low for the area you are in)
- "Insert trend here" + "insert relationship to real estate" For example: What Game of Thrones taught me about the real estate market

A quick Google search for "best real estate subject lines" will quickly reveal countless other ideas for getting your emails opened. Just remember, whatever your subject line is must in some way tie into your actual content. Nobody likes a tease.

Don't Tease. Be Relevant. Be Concise:
Once you have a killer subject line to lure people in, make sure that the content in your email is short, sweet, and to the point so that your recipients not only stay for long enough to digest what you are sending, but also so that it would be easy for them to take whatever action you are hoping for. It is mental anguish to get an email that is seven paragraphs long with no spacing and no formatting. I love emails that are two to three sentences long, and to the point. A good email doesn't give away the farm and all the info a potential recipient could want. It leaves them wanting more, so much more, that than they email you, call you, or take your other desired action.

Email Signature:

After the content itself a good or bad email signature can seal the deal or scrap it. Almost every mass email I have ever received has used an obnoxious crappy email signature that takes up half my screen. These signatures not only make the email look more like marketing but they make the email take longer to load. Half the time these signatures do not display correctly depending on the recipient's email provider, internet speed, or device type. Keep your signature as simple as your email. When in doubt stick with the basics.

Think about your email signature and think about how you can strip that down to the very minimum. What is important here?

• Name

• Title

• Company

• Phone Number

• Legally required compliance information that you might have

Do you really need to include your photo, logo, a tagline, a team name, a Bible passage, 3 emojis, video links, a cat gif, and some reviews in your signature every single time you send an email? I am not saying not to do it if these items are all important to you, I am just saying to be very careful because the more you add to your email signature, the more it may look like spam, the longer your email may take to load, and ultimately fewer people will end up seeing your content.

Warning: *If you are using an image file as your signature, make sure you also have a plain text version available. This way if your signature does not download on someone's phone or through some error your image doesn't display, your recipients will still have some contact information for you.*

PRO TIP: *Your initial mass email went out and worked? Send it out again with a new subject line to the segment of people who you sent it to the first time but who didn't open it. Similarly, you can send it again to people who clicked the link inside your email. The idea here is to try again with those who didn't open the first time or to try again with people who are interested (because they opened or clicked) but didn't take further action. If you are looking for a real world comparison, think of this like how Amazon or an online retailer would email you if you put something in your shopping cart but didn't end up buying.*

For this "2nd email" I usually try to change my subject line a little bit. I might do Re: following up, or something of that nature just to make people think it's a reply and that they missed the original. If you are already putting the time into the content and figuring out who you want to send it too, sending a second email to the people that did not open it the first is kind of a no-brainer. Tangible things you can add on to your strategy without adding on to your mental energy or physical costs are always a win.

Tangible Things To Stop Doing Now

As many of the chapters in this book illustrate, improving your business usually requires tangible work and action. Although it may seem counter-intuitive, there are also ways to improve your results that require the opposite of action, they instead requite that you simply stop or modify things you are doing that may be hurting you or your chances of success.

Many of us have heard the saying "marketers ruin everything". Many people may even think that marketers have ruined the medium of email. These generalizations become more and more true every day because of un-savvy marketers (real estate professionals included) who use email marketing to send out content that is often both too frequent, too irrelevant, or formatted in an unreadable way. Since we already covered a few tangible ideas when it comes to email marketing we decided to add a list of No-No's as well. Feel free to scan the list to make sure you aren't doing any of these things, or simply read it for laughs because I'm sure many of us have made fun of our poor colleagues who market these ways.

Stop sending newsletters that you or your team didn't create.
It's hard enough for people to craft newsletters that are relevant to people they know well, it's even harder if not impossible for an online company with millions of customers to craft newsletters that are relevant to anyone.

Stop sending out emails with pictures of homes that are clearly not in your area.
I live in Michigan. It's cold and frigid here 60% of the year. We don't have palm trees. Stop sending me emails with pretty pictures of houses that have palm trees, ocean views, and southern style roofs. First of all, don't add photos just to make things pretty, only add photos when they add value.

Stop putting the word "newsletter" in your subject line.

When the word newsletter is in your subject line you have already lost 90% of anyone who is remotely busy. Get creative.

Stop personalizing emails with bad mail merged data.

If you have someone's first name in your CRM in ALL CAPS and you go to insert the 'First Name' using a mass merge it will display to your client in all caps as well. It's a surefire way for clients to realize that your otherwise great email wasn't personalized.

Stop sending emails out where the greeting is in a different font/color/size than the rest of the email.

Another key giveaway that you sent a spam email, or that you, in general, are sloppy and don't have attention to detail (something I am desperately trying to improve on myself) is when your salutation is in a font that doesn't match the rest of your email. Always send yourself a preview email before you send it to others and check out how it looks visually.

Stop importing your entire list of every human you have ever emailed.

Garbage in. Garbage out. If you download a list of every person who you have ever emailed and who has emailed you and then upload that to your CRM to email all of them — just don't bother. It will be impossible to send a mass email out to this entire group of randoms that offers any value to anyone. We can all agree that it is pretty annoying when someone starts spamming you and your only communication with them was 4 years ago for something unrelated.

SECTION 16

CTAs

———

One important thing to talk about when you are doing any marketing, email or otherwise, is a call-to-action (CTA). A CTA is effectively the part of your message or content that convinces someone to take one of your desired actions. It is important to be strategic about where you place your CTA's, as well as to also offer different types of actions they could complete depending on their current stage in the customer life cycle. Although all forms of marketing have calls to action, emails are an especially great medium because you are sending customers a message that can have live links to click, call, or reply. For companies trying to sell something, the CTA is often to get someone to click to buy, but for real estate sales professionals, often simply getting a reply is the goal. When crafting your CTA's and placing them in an email always consider what the total end goal is.

If your end goal is to get someone to buy a house with you, or sign a mortgage application, remember to always use CTA's that will get people from their current stage in the home buying process or customer life cycle, to a stage that gets them closer to the closing table. For instance, if you are marketing to old Zillow leads, you already know they are interested in homes, and you may even know what types of homes they are interested in. With this knowledge you can craft a call to action in your email to get them either lists of homes to look at that are similar to their interest, or you can present a different CTA to offer a quick pre-approval before interest rates go up. The offer for a pre-approval is a natural next progression if you already know they are looking at homes, and the pre-approval with the mention of higher rates gives them a reason to complete your action now rather than waiting.

I challenge you to think about the end goals that you would like to accomplish in your email and other types of marketing. Is the desired outcome of your email to get the recipient to go to your website, fill out a form, and become a lead? If so, make sure to consider the audience you are sending it to. If you already have their contact info (a good email address, phone number, etc..) and they have yours, getting them to fill out a form on your site only re-categorizes them as a newer lead but doesn't necessarily get you a new lead. Sometimes making your CTA or desired action simply getting a reply to your email can work incredibly well for real estate professionals because of the simplicity, and low level of complication. If you make your call to action an action that's easy to complete, more people will complete it.

DOUBLING UP ON VALUE

———

One of the saddest realizations I had a few years ago was when I looked back at some of the marketing pieces and blogs I had spent hours creating, only to see the real statistics that close to nobody was looking at the fruits of my hard work. As I started talking to other colleagues who were also doing a lot on social media and their websites, we noticed a trend: lots of blogs and/or videos but very view impressions[22] or views.

This was an eye-opener. My team and I had spent so much time on creating content but so little time on disseminating it. Even the best and most well thought out articles, videos, and content cannot generate you leads unless you market them. Ever since then we have put together what we call a content dissemination plan for every piece we make. For example, each time we make a blog we pick at least 3 of our email groups to send it out to with a short description of why it is relevant to them. We then schedule it to go out again to the same group 3 weeks later with a subject line of "in case you missed it." We'll also schedule the same post to go out on any relevant social media sites, both now and 6 weeks out. Since rolling out this simple dissemination strategy we increased viewership, as well as action, on our content. The extra work required to do this has been less than 15 minutes per piece of content.

The tangible takeaway is simple. If you put time into creating something, put time into getting it out there as well. When the cost is the same, amplify your results in any way you can.

[22] Impressions: number of people who visited the page.

SELLING A BETTER VERSION OF YOU

———

Standing Out In A Crowded Market

Standing Out When You Aren't There

We have talked a lot about new things you can do, new ways to farm, new emails to send out, but what about things you are already doing that you can just do a little differently?

What is your ridiculously awesome competitive differential? If you are in real estate sales you are a sales person. Regardless of the area you work in, you are in a city full of other sales people selling exactly what you sell. Sure, you might have a secret sauce that you think makes you better than the next guy, but until a client experiences it, it's irrelevant. Once you can honestly and quickly explain the value you bring to the table to yourself, you can start to market it to others, and weave it into all aspects of your business.

TANGIBLE ACTIVITY:

Answer the below questions right here in the book or in whatever tool you are using to take notes.

1. **What makes you different from other people who do what you do in your area?**

2. **What makes you different from other people who do what you do at your office/branch/brokerage?**

3. **What makes you different from all other people who do what you do?**

4. **What are all of the services you provide clients that are of value?** This list should be long. Include even the smallest things. Even if it's something you only do for some clients as needed.

5. **Of the services you offer that provide value, which ones would customers not receive from one of your colleagues or competitors?**

6. Of the services you provide which ones can not be replaced by technology?
IE: when the robots take over, which ones will clients still need you for?

7. Which pieces of value that you provide do you think customers most value?

8. What do you do to make your value stand out and be known in the marketplace?

If you answered the above homework questions honestly and carefully you should be left with a few pieces of value that you offer, that customers care about, that you either do better than anyone else or are unique to you.

If you answered any questions with an "I don't know" or you finished reading it with a sense of fear that you don't market your value or yourself to the level you should, the next section offers some easy tips to get noticed (literally).

Now that you understand the value that you're truly offering, call, text, or email 10 past clients (or friends who are home owners) per month and ask what the most valuable part of using a Realtor was for them. This will help you to ensure that the value that you are offering aligns with what the majority of your customers are looking for.

Standing Out In A Crowded Market

What makes you a better choice than the other sales person who has roughly the same demographic profile as you and is likely less than a quarter of a mile away?

Hopefully, the unique value propositions that you figured out above partially answer that question. But standing out among similar competitors in a crowded market is often one of the most challenging dilemmas for real estate industry sales people. Luckily there are just as many ways to stand out and to be present as there are potential customers out there, because the method of standing out that you choose will get you noticed by a certain type of customer. As you formulate ways that you can stand out better, think about your niche, and the areas you want to be more prominent. What kinds of people stand out? What do they wear? What do they do differently? Why did you notice them?

One of the best ways to stand out in a crowded market is to market the details. Things that everyone is doing, or that all people in your profession offer are hard to market because they aren't exciting. The details of who you are, what you are into, and the quirky habits and hobbies you have are the best ways to stand out and get remembered.

People don't want to work with me because I know information about marketing. Who cares? You can Google marketing information. You can Google half the things in this book and figure out a way to apply them to real estate. Customers want to work with you because of the more granular details that they can resonate with. You went to such and such college, you were in the such and such club, you have a kid the that plays this or that sport/activity, you go to the same little coffee shop as them every single day, your parents both were social workers, etc.

TANGIBLE ACTIVITY:

Take all of your fun hobbies, dreams, some fun past experiences, education, experi-ences and write them down. Then send what you came up with to you your spouse/ best friend/ close colleague to see what they would add about you based on how they perceive you. These details and are what make you, you. These are the real reasons people would choose you over someone else, and at the end of the day, these are the details you need to sell.

Whether you are brand new to sales or have been around forever, a key action item is to take the items above (the fun details about you) and to turn them into a short 2-3 paragraph bio. This will be a piece that you can use both digitally as an email or on online profiles like your website/LinkedIn, as well as something you can hand out in print to potential customers.

All of the fun details in your bio are best thought of as little hooks that can keep people interested in you and your story and help them to develop connections with you. This is what's really going to set you apart and make you different from the 3,000 other people who do exactly what you do in your community. Once you take the time to make a bio, make sure you're putting it in all the right places. If you're a Realtor/lender, maybe Zillow, maybe your local association page, your company provided website, your own website, but also make a printout. Have this be the start of your listing packet. Have this be a part of your buyer packet. If you're a lender, have this be the start of the folder or email that you give to agents.

PRO TIP: *Once you have a solid bio written you can take the same content and make a short video. A video will engage people in a different way and can be more easily shared to social media. Remember, in the age of smartphones, videos don't have to be expensive, and you don't need to be a classically trained actor, as long as you can keep the video short (30 seconds to 2 minutes). Videos themselves are more shareable and give your raving fans a better way to share your personality with their connections. Once you do have a short bio video recorded you can include a link to it in your email signature. It can say "Meet Me", and link viewers to the video on YouTube or your website. I find that having a video in my email signature is especially helpful for when I am meeting with people who don't know me well, or what I look like. Having the video in my signature lets them figure out which guy at the coffee shop/bar is the one they are meeting with.*

Once you have a great bio, you're off to a good start. Next thing you'll need is a good headshot! Did one 2 years ago—do it again! In 2019 it is pretty impossible to not have a headshot at all. But it is very possible to not have a great one. If you are currently using a headshot from more than 2 years ago, it is time to schedule a reshoot. A headshot needs to be a reflection of you today, not who you used to be. A good headshot is a preview signal to your clients of how well you're going to make their house look when you list it, your ability to judge quality in a home you are showing them, or your level of professionalism and credibility when issuing a pre-approval letter. Make sure that all the photos that you use on your website and on your online media are appropriate and high quality. If you have a professional photographer at your office, email them now to schedule a shoot. Don't have a photographer at your disposal? Try asking the person who takes your listing photos, or post on social media that you are looking for a connection to someone with a good camera. Once you have the photos, request versions that are cropped specifically for the various places you want to use them: Zillow, your Realtor association website, your website... etc. A great photo that is stretched or pixelated because of how a website formats it will not do you any favors when trying to win clients.

It would be easier if real estate professionals could just present their best selves when working digitally. Even though so much of the real estate transaction itself happens digitally, over 40% of all buyers and sellers found their agent through traditional word of mouth referrals[23]. This means that professionals looking to stand out, need to focus on the real world as well. This is often easier said than done for many because where online you can choose to showcase your great bio, photo some links and press save, in real life you have to do it all the time. It has to become a part of you.

Sure, some of standing out in real life is pure personality, tone of voice, and overall levels of boisterousness and gravitas/charisma. These attributes can't necessarily be changed as easily or simply be turned on and off. The real opportunities for getting noticed face to face will often be in what you wear and how you present yourself.

The good news is that anyone, in any price range or area, can wear things that are bright, or that stand out a little. The hard part is that the level to which you need to "amplify your brightness" will depend on your surroundings. If you are going to a networking event where everyone already dresses to stand out, you may need to get creative. Similarly, if you are going to church on a Sunday you may not want to wear your bright pink tuxedo with matching feather boa, even if it worked great for attracting eyeballs at last year's Christmas party.

Traditionally, I have seen female sales people perfect the art of subtly standing out much better than guys, who sometimes end up standing out like a sore thumb. One way of subtly getting noticed would be to wear accessories that will garner eyeballs, rather than an entire outfit. Think jewelry, shoes, ties, socks, cufflinks, suit jackets, handbags, briefcases, watches etc.

I'm not saying to always be the most ostentatious person in the room, but I am saying that a good sales person shouldn't blend into the walls. One example of a trick I have been using for years is to wear business casual shoes that have a bright colored sole. I have been wearing Cole Haan shoes[24] for the past five years and I'm absolutely 'raving fan' level obsessed with them. Cole Haan has numerous lines of business appropriate shoes that come in bright colors, fun fabrics, and most importantly comfortable (even athletic) fits. They're absolutely fantastic because no one is expecting someone to walk into a professional conference or lunch meeting wearing a pair of black leather shoes on top of a bright yellow sole. I call them my networking line of shoes, and consistently meet 1-2 new people every time I wear them. I'm a firm believer that anytime you can wear something that is

---

[23] The average open rate for real estate is 19%. https://mailchimp.com/resources/email-marketing-benchmarks
[24] If you need a visual: https://www.colehaan.com

noticeable yet still appropriate, more people will talk to you. In an industry where every conversation is an at-bat and way to stay top of mind, why wouldn't you add some fun splashes to your swagger and up the conversation count?

If you are thinking about giving this tip a try but feel like it is a little bit outside of your comfort zone, try to use a holiday as a way to ease into it. Holidays (especially Christmas/Halloween) are almost like free days when it's completely appropriate to add some seasonal flair to your attire. Although you may not get noticed as much by standing out visually during the holidays, you still have a big opportunity to increase your conversation count due to the sheer number of parties and events that cluster around any day off work.

Especially in our industry, there are happy hours starting December 1st and Christmas parties going all the way up to February 1st (the new trends seems to be doing Christmas parties after Christmas to give people a break, when sometimes all this does is extends the season of constant parties). There are a million events, so what can you do? What can you buy that's going to help you stand out? I've personally been wearing a Christmas suit, a very festive, ornamental, sometimes light up, Christmas suit for the past three years. Every year, I try to buy a new one. Every time I walk into a party, I get laughed at, I get mocked by my friends, and I get compliments from hundreds of people. The reason I do it is that it gets a little bit of attention. It gets people to come up and talk to me, who might have otherwise not had anything to say. In our world of constantly being on our phones and devices all many people want is a reason to come and say hi to you. If you have something on your physical person that gives them that reason, it's a win/win. Plus, it's festive.

Standing out isn't just for parties and large events, it's also for everyday life. When was the last time you actually talked to someone in line at Starbucks or while trapped in an elevator? The places that standing out often works best are ones like that, where you have a captive audience of bored people waiting around.

 Get off your phone when you are in public. When you are eyes down, staring at a phone that doesn't really love you back (sorry Siri) you are telling the world that you are closed for conversation. By replacing your downward gaze with a forward facing smile (but not an overly excited smile, because that would just be creepy) you are increasing the chances that others will engage with you.

Standing Out When You Aren't There

Standing out while you are going about your daily activities and events is a great way to amplify your networking opportunities for leads, but after a while and a certain amount of success we all become limited by the same factor, time.

Although it is always possible to hire an assistant or team member to free up your time, it is still important to stand out and be remembered even when you aren't around. This brings us to one of the simplest chapters in the book: swag.

Swag
noun

1. Promotional merchandise with logos and relevant information that can be given out to promote a brand, corporate identity, or event.

This is one area where real estate sales people have actually been excelling for years. Coffee mugs, knives, shovels, pens, etc. have all been used successfully by agents and lenders as promotional leave behinds that help to keep sales people top of mind for longer.

The key thing to remember when you decide to buy swag with your logo, is that it only helps your business if you order the right products, for the right people, and disseminate them at the right times and places. Think about products you can logo up that people will actually get use out of, or products that have some sort of wow factor. Products that people will be excited to use even if they have a small promotional logo on them. Also, think about products people are okay with advertising being on, and ones they won't be okay with. Certain products are situational; consider the example of a beach towel. Customers are unlikely to be excited to receive a beach towel at closing with your logo plastered all over it. That being said, if you showed up to a free public event where people were sitting on the lawn/beach, passing out logo'd towels that people could use right then and there you could quickly become a hero, and people might even line up to get your swag.

Below are some examples of sales person swag that we have seen them use successfully to stay top of mind.

Pens: *Pens are some of the cheapest items to buy, but be sure to buy good ones. A tangible, easy strategy is to drop off a box of your pens to every restaurant in town that you frequent. Waitresses constantly need pens after annoying customers steal* them, and they would rather help to advertise you than buy their own pens. A few local agents I work with do this well by delivering pens to restaurants in their farm areas once a month. They consistently hear back from customers and people in the community that their pens are everywhere. Since perception is reality, if people think you are a big deal, you are.

Winter Shovels: *This only applies to cold weather states but many lenders and agents will give away snow scrapers and shovels. Items that are very handy but that you never think to go and buy. Especially for customers closing on a home in mid-fall, the shovel you brought them might come in handy when that first snow storm comes. Logos can often be added via stickers on the handle or the shovel itself.*

The Coffee Mug: *Coffee mugs typically have some staying power if they are high quality. They get used over and over, and many sales people who pass out custom mugs at closing see them in clients houses when they come back to relist the homes years later. Another tangible strategy is to find local diner style restaurants (typically breakfast/lunch joints) that use business and promotional mugs to save costs. This isn't as common as it used to be, but when you do find a restaurant that will let you give them your mugs for use at their establishment, your mugs will get a ton of shelf life and attention. A special bonus here would be to make your mug stand out with something a little bit funny or a call to action.*

USB Flash Drives: *These are fairly cheap and easy to customize with your infor-mation. Some sales people will give clients flash drives at closing with copies of all of their transaction information. These typically end up being saved because you pre-loaded them with something of value.*

A Must Have Product: *Every year some product comes out that everybody wants. Whether it's a YETI mug or a fidget spinner, if you can tap into the hot item of the year and brand them with your logo, you may even have people begging for your freebies. A colleague and friend who did YETI mugs as branded swag a few years ago has had pictures of his logo'd YETI instagrammed around the world, and still regularly receives requests from clients eager to replace a lost one.*

STAY SIMPLE.
STAY SUCCESSFUL.
KEEP EXECUTING.

———

It is not by accident that one of the last chapters in the book covers a concept like swag. On first glance, you could look at those paragraphs as ones to skip because on first glance they seem tried, tested, and in some cases tired ideas; however, their purpose in the book and specifically as an ending is to remind you that some of the best ideas are the ones that are simplest to execute. When in doubt, just do something. The best sales people aren't always the ones looking to constantly innovate and reinvent the wheel. Most often the people you are chasing, are the ones who find simple ideas, put their spin on them, and execute them time and time again. It can be very easy in a commission based business to spend all of your time "innovating" and trying to always be the first one on to the next big thing; however, 9 times out of 10 we see the most profitable and happy sales people being the ones who choose strategies that are simple, executable, and replicable. Most importantly these agents choose strategies that they enjoy.

If you are like me and tend to learn best when the messages and ideas are tangible, make hunting for tangible ideas your goal every day. Rather than going to a conference and taking 30 pages of notes that you will never look back on, simply keep a record of tangible and executable ideas you come across that seem within your wheelhouse. Learn to be discerning of people trying to sell you on their success without sharing any exact details of what they did to get there. Ask tangible and specific questions, and keep digging when the answers or presentations you hear don't paint a clear enough picture. It's not that people who don't explain enough aren't doing a good job, but if it's your time being spent listening, then it is in your best interest to ask those probing questions to get what you need out of every learning opportunity. By staying curious when others describe what's working for them, you can continue to build on the tangible tips in this book and further develop a guide of action items that will take your business where you want it to go.

What to do once you have tried all of the tangible items in this book that sparked your interest? Stay curious — all the time. See new software? Investigate it. See an agent or lender who appears to be experiencing success, or rising at a good pace? Take them to lunch. Be curious. Ask questions. Set goals. Stay hungry.

Now TAG, you're it.

Almost every month since I began writing this book, levels of housing inventory around the country have gone down. If you want to get more closings, you in part need more total listings in your market to sell to your clients. Now that you are "it" — send a link to this book to a few friends in the industry so they too can use the same tangible tips to generate some new listings for all of us. In our industry, mutual success creates more opportunity for all of us.

ABOUT THE AUTHOR

Matt Muscat is passionate about great marketing, great people, great food, and great world travel adventures! While earning his bachelors and masters degrees from Michigan State University, he studied the digital side of marketing and developed a deep passion for making the complex, simple in the world of marketing. As the Marketing Director at Treadstone Funding, one of the nation's top boutique mortgage lenders, Matt has had the opportunity to meet and exchange ideas with professionals in all areas of residential real estate. He has been able to collaborate on the best marketing methods and practices with some of the top lenders and top real estate professionals in the country and create fantastic ways to leverage specific techniques to increase sales. As the Founder/Owner of Maltese Marketing, a digital marketing firm headquartered in Grand Rapids, Matt and his team have served clients in 38 states and 4 countries, and have helped them to advance their digital and other marketing efforts to create tangible results. Matt is an adjunct professor of digital marketing at a local university and is often available (especially if the location is warm) to speak to groups of all sizes. Matt has an amazingly supportive wife and young son, who are also his favorite accomplices for trips of all kinds, during which they enjoy checking out new and far away restaurants.

Please visit mattmuscat.com for monthly updates on new Tangible Action Guide Strategies.

ACKNOWLEDGMENTS

This book could not have been possible if it were not for the help, guidance, and time of countless people who I connected with over the past 5 years. TAG began as a collection of notes that I used as a way of organizing all of the advice that my team and I would give to sales professionals in meetings and presentations. First and foremost a huge thank you to Kevin Polakovich and Brendan O'Driscoll who took a chance on me and brought me into the real estate industry in 2011 — thank you both for truly being the best mentors that someone growing their career could ask for. Second a big thank you to my graphic designer, Kari Radermacher, whose designs and careful editing helped turn TAG from a rough word document into something that actually looks like a book! Thanks to all of the others who helped me to edit and proofread as well, without you I wouldn't sound nearly as intelligent. Thanks to my amazing wife and family whose support and positive vibes kept this project going when a sunny day made me want to pause and lie in the sun with a cocktail. Finally thanks to all of the many Realtors, lenders, colleagues, and co-workers who have sat down with me over the past 9 years. It is from the wisdom that these people shared with me in various meetings that I was able to learn, adapt, and create strategies that will help us all grow.

Made in the USA
Coppell, TX
28 February 2020

16314203R00085